I0664999

UNLOCKING SECRETS

How to Get People to Tell You Everything

Dr David Craig
International Undercover Expert

Skyhorse Publishing

Copyright © 2013 Dr. David Craig

First Skyhorse Publishing Edition 2018

All rights reserved. No part of this book may be reproduced in any manner without the express written consent of the publisher, except in the case of brief excerpts in critical reviews or articles. All inquiries should be addressed to Skyhorse Publishing, 307 West 36th Street, 11th Floor, New York, NY 10018.

Skyhorse Publishing books may be purchased in bulk at special discounts for sales promotion, corporate gifts, fund-raising, or educational purposes. Special editions can also be created to specifications. For details, contact the Special Sales Department, Skyhorse Publishing, 307 West 36th Street, 11th Floor, New York, NY 10018 or info@skyhorsepublishing.com.

Skyhorse® and Skyhorse Publishing® are registered trademarks of Skyhorse Publishing, Inc.®, a Delaware corporation.

Visit our website at www.skyhorsepublishing.com.

10 9 8 7 6 5 4 3 2 1

Library of Congress Cataloging-in-Publication Data is available on file.

Cover design by Michael Short

Print ISBN: 978-1-5107-3077-9
E-Book ISBN: 978-1-5107-3078-6

Printed in the United States of America

I would like to dedicate this book to the those whose lives have been touched by cancer. Their quality of life and the challenges they face in their individual fight against this sickness are greatly assisted by the researchers who work tirelessly to find cures and better treatment alternatives, by medical specialists who care for them every day and by good hearted people who donate their time and money in support of this cause.

I greatly admire the courage of the victims of this illness and their supporting families. None more so than the Neave family who have fought against a rare and aggressive mutant cancer gene (BRCA2) that has already taken their great grandmother and grandmother. The two older Neave sisters, Veronica and Chrissy, have so far avoided the gene's attack by undertaking radical surgery. The third sister, Elisha, and their mother, Claudette, have not been so lucky and for them the fight is on in earnest.

This book is dedicated to the Neave family and others who find themselves in a similar fight for life.

TABLE OF CONTENTS

Washington DC, 2000

It was November 2000; four months since I had completed a doctorate in Covert Operations, which was the culmination of several years spent researching undercover tactics and the people who undertake clandestine operations. At that stage, I had also spent a decade with the Australian Federal Police in a number of countries and various roles—many of which were covert.

I had just finished an undercover deployment in another country and had flown direct from there to Washington to assist with an undercover training course. Before I started the training, though, there was someone I wanted to meet. He was the first FBI undercover agent to successfully infiltrate the Mafia; his name then, was Joe D Pistone.

FBI undercover operation Sun-Apple had Joe living and working within the inner circle of the Miami and New York Mafia for six years. As a result of his gutsy and tenacious evidence gathering, 200 Mafia identities received hefty gaol terms for crimes ranging from extortion to murder. He had spent several years in witness protection and now continues to have a lifetime $500,000 Mafia contract on his head. He lives under a different name. Despite this, Hollywood still managed to make the movie *Donnie Brasco* about his exploits—Joe was played by Johnny Depp.

I wanted to meet Joe to learn from his experience and analyse why he, above all others, was so successful. The Mafia would like to meet Joe—but for a very different reason.

After I left the airport and made my way towards the meeting place, I conducted counter-surveillance drills to ensure I wasn't followed as I didn't want to bring any unwanted guests to our meeting. We met at an undisclosed location and I got right to the point . . .

I said, 'So, XXXX (name withheld), what were your biggest psychological assets when you were undercover for so long?'

He said, 'Well, Dave, you gotta know who you really are and what you stand for—and you gotta be able to get 'em to talk. If they don't talk you don't learn noth'n about 'em or what they do. You gotta be able to open them up.'

Having worked undercover, I knew how true that statement was. The angst and sacrifice of a covert operation was worth nothing if you came out with zip! I spent some time with XXXX, listening and learning from his well-tested undercover modus operandi.

Now after 22 years as a sworn federal law enforcement officer and 8 years as a covert operations consultant and trainer to government agencies and corporate entities. I would like to share some of the most successful interpersonal techniques I learned during that time. In *Unlocking Secrets*, I have translated the highly advanced methods used by spies and covert operatives to learn secret information, and show you how you can use these skills in everyday professional and personal situations. These skills will provide you with a distinct psychological edge in business, professional and personal relationships—beyond what has been openly taught before.

Unlocking Secrets is the second in my *Psychological Edge* series of books and builds on the first book in the series, *Lie Catcher; Become a Human Lie Detector in Under 60 Minutes*.[1] These books complement each other; the first book assists to identify when a person lies and hides information from you, and *Unlocking Secrets* allows you to access that very information. But it isn't necessary to have read the first book to learn and apply the techniques in this book.

When you have read this book, and practised the techniques, you will be able to better understand and influence people, and others will 'open up' to you and tell you information they would not usually divulge—and do it willingly.

Read on and reap the benefits these unique skills can provide. Good luck!

INTRODUCTION

People hide information from others for a variety of reasons—some are harmless and some are not. The information hidden from us is secret and in many circumstances it can be to our advantage to know that information. Spies and undercover operatives have been successfully getting people to reveal secret information for many years. In the following pages I reveal the techniques that these specialists use to extract information so that you can apply them just as effectively to everyday personal and professional situations. These advanced interpersonal communication skills will give you an unprecedented psychological edge.

Have you ever been in a situation where you just know someone isn't giving you all the information? It may be a child, a client, a partner, a business colleague or a competitor. This book will provide you with the knowledge and the practical skills required to have people willingly share that hidden secret information with you.

You may have been attracted to this book because a person has kept information hidden from you in the past which ultimately hurt, disappointed or disadvantaged you—or someone close to you. Perhaps you need to learn hidden information to improve the way you manage:

- Children or students

- Prospective clients

- Patients or partners

- Business competitors

You can also use hidden information to:

- Create new contacts

- Improve networking

- Meet that special someone—yes, these skills can help with dating and even enrich existing relationships!
- Engage and influence people to improve your personal and business relationships

Accessing secrets is the key to achieving all these. But secrets are just that—secret. Secrets are a fascinating subject and we usually feel privileged when someone shares their most secret of secrets with us. Sometimes though, people hide information from us that we could use to better protect ourselves and our relationships, support the secret-keeper (in the case of a child, client or patient issue), and use to our business advantage. In *Part One* I tell you all about secrets—why people keep secrets, and the effects of keeping and revealing secrets.

Its aim is not to give you the skills to harm or embarrass people by getting them to reveal their secrets, but to benefit and protect them and you. Uncovering hidden information can liberate a person, assist with welfare management, and provide much needed information to medical professionals, lawyers, teachers and parents. It can also strengthen a negotiating position, provide a market advantage, increase sales and provide a psychological edge in the workplace.

Out with the Old and in with the New

In the early 1980s body language was the new frontier of interpersonal communications and there was an explosion of information about it. Books on the subject charted new ground and greatly enhanced people's understanding of interpersonal communication. Knowing about body language provided a fantastic advantage and insight to possessors of this 'new knowledge'. Now, however, there are literally hundreds of books on this subject and how it may be applied to our everyday lives. Some people seek to replicate or fake body language signals to gain an advantage or give a false impression. There are even training courses on how to do exactly that!

The new frontier for motivated people with a thirst for knowledge and who want to improve their interpersonal communication is found in the understanding, development and application of advanced psychological skills. These skills don't negate the need to understand body language, but with so many people knowledgeable in that area, we need to look elsewhere for that interpersonal communication edge. We're well into the 21st century and it's about time that our interpersonal mind techniques caught up with our interpersonal body techniques!

The new frontier is no longer the physical as body language was—it's now the psychological.

Getting 'Em to Talk—Elicitation

In *Part Two* I tell you about elicitation. The term 'elicitation' is used extensively by government intelligence agencies, covert operatives and undercover agents to describe the subtle verbal extraction of information from persons of interest. In other words, 'elicitation unlocks hidden information'. The tactic of elicitation has been used for many years and continues today to be the main staple for gaining information by spy agencies' *defensive* and *offensive* intelligence programs.

For example, in 2001 I was working in the jungle border region that separates East Timor and Indonesia. At that time there were active militia groups on the Indonesian side of the border who were conducting violent cross border raids into East Timor with devastating consequences for the civilian population. Using the knowledge I've included in *Parts One* and *Two* of this book and the practical skills from *Parts Three* and *Four*, I was able to elicit information from a border contact, who *unknowingly* provided me with enough information for HQ Intelligence to piece together the planned timing for the next raid. As a result, United Nations Peacekeepers were in place when the next raid took place and several militiamen were detained—and many civilians spared.

You may not have a need to use elicitation skills in such an extreme environment. However, *Unlocking Secrets* applies these very successful elicitation techniques to everyday situations. In *Part Three* I show you how to use effective interpersonal skills to engage people in conversation, get them to like you and ultimately open up to you. You can use these skills in situations such as when a child doesn't want to admit to you they have done something wrong, or when a person, patient or client has a deep and scarring secret that you need to access so you can provide them some much needed support. In business, it could be a competitor, a client, a colleague, your staff or your supervisor who has information that would provide you an advantage or much needed insight.

Elicitation will get you that information and *Unlocking Secrets* shows you how, using the easy-to-follow four steps of the READ Model of Elicitation, which I discuss in *Part Four*. Designed specifically for this book and released publicly for the first time, this very effective model simplifies an otherwise complex process and will guide you to learning the hidden information you need.

Comparatively, secret-keeping is an under-researched area and has always been a mine field of complex theoretical psychology. Even less is known about how to unlock a person's hidden information and much has been concealed behind a veil of secrecy by undercover agencies—until now. *Unlocking Secrets* takes the latest cutting edge theories and some of the most effective psychological tools from the cloak and dagger world of covert operations, and shows how they may be simply and effectively used to advantage in everyday situations.

Part One:

The Secret Nature of Secrets

This part of the book contains a necessary degree of theoretical information about why people keep information hidden—why they keep secrets. We are aiming to uncover hidden information and to successfully do this we need a requisite working knowledge of the theory behind secret-keeping. When unlocking hidden information we are dealing with varying human dynamics and psychological factors that vary from one person and their environment to the next.

The READ Model of Elicitation (explained in *Part Four*) will assist greatly with steering you through the elicitation process. However, without understanding why a particular person in a given circumstance is hiding information from you, you will only have half the picture. With a sound understanding of secret-keeping, you will be able to calibrate, tailor and be flexible with your elicitation strategies and as a result you'll be more successful.

Any information that is hidden from you is considered a secret. The very topic of secrets carries with it a certain mystique and intrigue in the minds of most people across most cultures. A quick internet search for 'secret' demonstrates this when it returns over 259 million results, ranging from 'secrets of keeping a happier dog' to 'government secrets revealed'. Secrets are something that everyone knows about, and many are interested in learning the hidden information of others.

The paparazzi chase, invade and provoke the rich and famous in an effort to uncover secret activities to satisfy an insatiable public thirst for the most recently uncovered information. The most desired activities it seems, are the ones the rich and famous try their hardest to hide—a break-up, a new romance, a health or drug issue or a well-hidden skeleton from the past. In pursuit of hidden information, some newspapers have even illegally intercepted the private phone calls of well-known people so they may learn secret information—information that *was* secret until they unveiled it.

Every day people stand around the water cooler, the lunch room, in coffee shops and bars discussing what others *may* be doing or who *may* be having an affair with whom, or what someone *may* have said, or done. The most prized information is, of course, secret information that no one else in the office knows. This brings with it power and advantage to those who possess it. Clearly, office gossip would die a quick death, as would gossip blogs and tabloid journalism, if people weren't interested in the hidden activities of others.

Commercially, secrets are kept to protect technological advancements, research programs and product formulas. Similarly, business and marketing strategies are kept from competing companies to maintain a competitive edge. Not infrequently, corporations will hide information that may cause shareholders concern such as impending corporate mergers or market share losses or sell-offs, in an effort to protect share prices (and perhaps the CEO's job!). Auctioneers vehemently protect reserve price information and retailers hide the *real* cost price of items. Secrets within stock markets are locked down by serious criminal consequences (insider trading) for those that divulge them.

Similarly, governments protect their information both from domestic disclosure and from the reach of other governments with laws, policies and intelligence agencies. The latter are also often charged with covertly learning the secrets of other governments, ranging from reserve trade prices (e.g. wheat, wool, minerals, etc.), to military intelligence. In a similar vein, intellectual property and corporate secrets are being proactively poached by other companies and also by competing governments, such as China.[2] There can be no dispute—there is big business in knowing the secrets of others.

Secrets are an elusive and very complex phenomena that are naturally a part of everyone's life; we all have secrets and it's natural that people want to keep some information hidden, or told to just a very few. While there seems to be a widely held interest in accessing hidden information, secrets and secrecy have not been researched as completely as many other areas. Some very credible studies have been undertaken in some areas; however, it remains a relatively under-researched area. There is also a lot of conjecture surrounding some areas that have been researched. Put simply, there is a lot we don't know about secrets and we know even less about how to unlock them.[3]

Spy agencies have known for decades that by using particular conversational skills in conjunction with often illegal incentive and pressuring tactics, they can get people to open up and reveal secrets they shouldn't. While we, as everyday law abiding citizens, still have a need to learn hidden information, we want to do this legally—and we can. Academic research has shown that under the correct circumstances people will share their hidden information with at least one other person, sometimes more.[4] This is primarily due to our natural urge to share or unload secret information—this is the usual human default position.[5] In *Part*

Two, we'll learn how to amplify a person's urge to share hidden information with you.

Some of the most common reasons people hide information are that they want to avoid being embarrassed, shunned or rejected by others; to avoid making a negative impression; or to avoid hurting another person's feelings. Interestingly, research has shown that people who divulge their secrets have a measurable improvement in their health.[6] Elicitation skills provide a capability to assist a person to share their hidden information so they may be better supported.

Regardless of whether we want to unlock hidden information for our business or personal advantage or to assist a person who is carrying a burdensome secret, we need to select the correct elicitation technique and remain flexible with our approach when using it. To enable us to do this successfully, it's necessary to have a closer look at the theory behind secret-keeping.

What is a Secret?

This sounds like quite a simple question and most people have an answer, as I did when I first commenced researching why people want to keep information hidden from others and how to unlock it. However, the more I read, the more I realized there was a myriad of different understandings of what an actual secret is. There was, and still remains, much conjecture in the academic, legal and professional arenas about what constitutes a secret.

Some people consider information is only secret if it is held exclusively by one person and not shared with anyone else; others that a secret is any information that is deliberately withheld from only one other person but all others may know. Some ask this question: Is information still classified as secret if the information is shared with more than one person? If so, and the information continues to be shared, at what point does it stop being 'a secret'? When five people know, perhaps ten or even fifty? There are even various legal precedents on this very point in different courts' jurisdictions, highlighting the conjecture around this seemingly simple question.

Other questions arise as we consider the subject in more detail. Some academics suggest that it is not only possible to keep a secret all *to* yourself—it is also possible to keep a secret from yourself. Now this may be starting to sound a bit ridiculous. However, Sigmund Freud suggested in 1915 that we have three levels of consciousness. *The Conscious Mind:* the one we use for our current thinking, focusing and processing information; *The Preconscious Mind:* the one that is aware of things, but we are not focusing upon them—but can if we choose to; and *The Subconscious Mind:* the one that acts and thinks independently and beyond our control, influencing our personality and our behavior. More recent research has shown it is likely that the Subconscious Mind may in fact have even more influence over our behavior than first proposed by Freud.[7]

So, if you subscribe to that line of thinking, it certainly is possible that information may be suppressed in people's minds so deeply that it actually becomes a secret from themselves. Perhaps I've been keeping secrets from myself for years—that might also explain why so often I can't find the TV remote and my car keys!

On a serious note, when we are attempting to elicit information from a patient, client, child or partner, we need to be aware that it's possible that the information has been suppressed so very deeply that the person is unaware of its very existence. If during the conversation you suspect this to be the case, caution should be exercised as the recollection of deeply suppressed memories is often a very emotive event and qualified support and guidance is recommended.

As the focus of this book is the practical application of eliciting hidden information of benefit to you or those you care for, there is little point undertaking a philosophical analysis of the various theories that define secrecy. What we need is a practical and universal definition that we can keep in mind when unlocking this type of information. The most sensible and concise definition of secrecy, and one we'll rely on in this book, is that secrecy is simply 'the intentional concealment of information from "*others*".'[8] 'Others' may include entities such as businesses, corporations, clubs and governments and also people such as partners, children, friends, work colleagues, complete strangers and importantly you.

In addition to understanding the definition of a secret, there are also some frequently used terms in this book that are vital to understand when discussing secrets and elicitation. These are:

- **Secret-keeper**: A secret-keeper is a person or entity that has hidden information; the person or entity is keeping a secret.

- **Secret-target**: A person or entity who is intentionally not provided hidden information is called the 'secret-target,' as the person or entity is 'targeted' or disadvantaged by the secret. When a person or entity keeps information hidden from you—you are the secret-target; they are the secret-keeper.

Types of Secrets

While there remains much that we don't know about the nature of secrets, there have been several research projects undertaken by credible academics to better understand this subject. Confusingly, there are a myriad of different interpretations of the categories of secrets and the motivations for hiding information. If we want to elicit hidden information from a person, it assists greatly to know the type of secret the person has and the motivation for keeping the information from us.

Due to the diversity of interpretations, I have distilled all this information into two readily identifiable categories, making it easier to learn, identify and apply successful techniques. The two primary categories of secrets are self-focused and other-focused.

Self-Focused Secrets

Some people perceive an increasing and cumulative need to keep information hidden as they live their lives. Information is withheld or selectively released about their personal, professional, familial and financial matters to manipulate both their reputation and their relationships; sometimes justifiably so, sometimes not. While we may not have a *major* skeleton in the closet (no murders I hope!), most people reading this book would find they have some hidden information they would prefer others didn't know about. This is both understandable and normal.

Self-focused secrets can be defined as information that is kept secret by the secret-keeper with the view to some self-benefit. Self-focused secrets are information that, if made known, would result in a detrimental impact upon the secret-keeper such as embarrassment, an undesirable perception of the secret-keeper by others, or a loss of advantage or power.

The change in perception or loss of advantage may be totally justified or unjustified. For example, a person may keep secret the fact that they were at

6

some stage declared bankrupt. If this information is revealed it may cause embarrassment and fairly or unfairly change the way others perceive that person. It may be entirely appropriate for this information to remain hidden.

Unless, of course, you were planning to go into business with the person or lend the person money. In that case, you would have a right to know that information and if it were successfully kept secret from you, it could be to your detriment. Unlocking this type of information using the skills in *Parts Three* and *Four* of this book may disadvantage the secret-keeper but better protect your interests.

There is an almost limitless number of self-focused secrets covering a broad spectrum of subject areas. The sheer diversity of these types of secrets was highlighted in a study conducted at the University of Michigan.[9] In this study reported secrets ranged from minor: 'My father is an alcoholic' and 'I can't always enjoy sex...' to high risk secrets such as 'I'm constantly toying with the idea of killing myself' and '... I sometimes feel I have to (want to), (need to) kill another person,' and 'I have had incestuous relations with a member of my family'. The latter examples demonstrate how the secret-keeper or others may be better supported or protected if a family member, friend, medical professional were able to successfully elicit this hidden information.

Additionally, it may be information that a secret-keeper doesn't want to share with others as it is to their advantage to hold onto that knowledge—the secret provides an edge that would be lost if shared. For example, a student may learn that a particular question is on an impending exam paper, or a job applicant is informed of 'what the interview panel is looking for,' or a business may learn some 'inside' information about price tendered by a company competing for the same contract—to share this information would be disadvantageous; so a self-focused secret is kept.

The purpose of this book is not to pass judgement or provide a moral compass for people on when and when not to use these secret-revealing skills; this is a matter for the reader and the many different circumstances where these skills may be applied. On some occasions assisting a person to divulge their self-focused secret can provide an opportunity to better assist, support, protect or treat the person, e.g. a child being bullied at school or stalked/groomed by an internet predator, a victim of domestic violence, drug or alcohol addiction, etc.

Examples of self-focused secrets include:

- The number of car accidents a person has had
- A professional mistake in the workplace
- A failed business venture
- A socially awkward family situation or personal incident
- A tragic event that is painful to recall
- Infidelity
- Being abused as a child, or partner
- Addictions or use of illegal or prescribed drugs, or alcohol
- Eating disorders
- Conviction for a criminal offence
- Being the victim of a crime
- Having a phobia, such as an intense fear of flying, needles, spiders or snakes
- A person's financial situation, such as income, assets, liabilities and loans (credit card debt is a common self-focused secret—sometimes even between partners!)
- Business plans and marketing strategies
- Product information and corporate intelligence

In summary, self-focused secrets are kept to benefit or protect the secret-keeper, in most cases to avoid negative social consequences or to protect a personal or financial advantage. Now we'll discuss the second category of secrets—other-focused secrets—and the important subcategories of professional and personal other-focused secrets.

Other-Focused Secrets

Other-focused secrets, as the name suggests, are kept by a secret-keeper for the benefit of another person or entity. Other-focused secrets are kept by individuals and also entities such as companies, organisations and governments. The one primary distinction that sets this category apart from all others is *good intent*. Other-focused secrets have a 'good will' theme running through the motivation behind keeping the information hidden. This may be to protect another person or their feelings, or the company, the business, or the government the secret-keeper works for or is loyal to.

The 'good will' associated with this category of secret is exemplified within the medical profession. With the betterment of the patient in mind, medical professionals are, on occasion, placed in very difficult positions in respect to the disclosure of medical information.

For example, a patient may be receiving treatment for an illness that will most likely be terminal. In discussions between the doctor and the patient, the doctor may provide reported examples where people with a similar condition have made a full recovery. The doctor may keep secret that this is an extremely rare outcome and in his/her opinion, there is very little likelihood the patient will survive. This information is kept secret from the patient to provide hope, comfort and motivation for recovery. This is a professional other-focused secret

A real example that demonstrates both the difficulties for medical staff who are asked to keep an other-focused secret and the tragic consequences of not sharing a secret, albeit with the best intention, relates to a paediatric HIV/AIDS nurse who was working in a clinic in New Jersey.[10] The nurse was specifically requested by the mother of an infected eight-year-old girl to keep the nature of the infection secret from her daughter (the patient). The nurse and a social worker were concerned that the young girl would overhear comments made in the ward and this would reveal the true nature of the girl's illness, so they tried to persuade the mother to tell her daughter. The mother, trying to protect the daughter from this terrible news, refused and reinforced her wish that the girl not be informed. Sometime later when the nurse was making her rounds the young girl beckoned to her. The nurse leaned over so she could hear, as the girl was now very weak and it took some effort for her to speak. 'I am very sick,' she said. 'I think I have AIDS. But you have to promise. Don't tell my mother. It's a secret and she would be sad if she found out.' In this unfortunate situation, the nurse, the mother and the child were all unnecessarily burdened with an other-focused secret.

The concept of protecting another person in some way can be taken too far even with the best of intentions, so that not sharing their other-focused secret means the secret-

target (the person whom they are trying to protect by hiding information) becomes a victim of the good intention.

Some professions vehemently protect their other-focused (trade) secrets and there is a good reason for this, as their commercial viability can depend directly upon this information remaining secret; sometimes these secrets are protected for decades. Why would a company rely on using a secret to protect their product instead of using legal avenues such as trademark, intellectual property laws or patents? The reason for this is that company secrets can be protected indefinitely by secrets whereas patents and other legal mechanisms usually have a finite life span.

For example, in many countries patents lose their protection after 20 years.[11] Had Coca-Cola initially used a patent to protect its formula, the secret would have been unprotected public knowledge for over 50 years.[12] As such, Coca-Cola has successfully protected its secret for decades, though this has not been without its challenges. The seriousness of divulging commercially held secrets was brought home to a Coca-Cola secretary in 2006, when she stole documents and a liquid sample of the new Coke formula and attempted to sell the secrets to PepsiCo. PepsiCo contacted the Federal Bureau of Investigation (FBI), which launched an undercover investigation and charged three people. The secretary, Joya Williams, was sentenced in 2007 to eight years gaol. US Attorney David Nahmias said, 'Theft of valuable trade secrets will not be tolerated, not by the Justice Department and not even by competitors, as this case shows.'[13]

Other-focused secrets also occur in our personal lives, but are still selfless by nature. That is, the secret-keeper will protect the secret-target (the person from whom the secret is kept) often for years, by keeping information secret purely out of good will and intention. An example of this occurs when a married couple who decide they are no longer compatible and should separate, stay together for the sake of the children. This information is often hidden with the view to benefiting the couple's children.

There are also many light-hearted examples where other-focused secrets may only have a limited life, such as plans for a surprise birthday party or anniversary event, or secrets surrounding purchasing and hiding gifts. If you are a child—stop reading now! The biggest other-focused secret in the world is Santa or Father Christmas, who is even more popular than the Easter Bunny—the subject of the world's second biggest other-focused secret. If you are a child and still reading, you are now part of the world's biggest secrets. If you keep this information secret so you don't spoil the magic for other children then you are keeping an other-focused secret.

Examples of other-focused secrets include:
- Parents keeping a secret from a child that he/she was an 'accident'
- A friend telling you their hidden information, which if revealed would be damaging; you keep that information secret to protect your friend
- Surprise parties, gifts and awards
- The price of a gift to avoid embarrassing or making the receiver uncomfortable
- Military and police members keeping hazardous activities secret to save stress on their partners
- Customer and client lists, e.g. keeping details secret to protect the clients
- Product research results, e.g. kept secret by researchers for the benefit of the sponsoring company
- Doctor–patient and lawyer–client information
- Police informants and confidential sources, e.g. police protecting the identity of an informant to ensure the informant's safety
- Within the media; a journalist protecting the source of information and guaranteeing anonymity

The Function of Hiding Information

Depending upon your profession, family situation and circumstances you may aim to elicit information from a variety of people ranging from young children to adults. Elicitation techniques that work on children won't work on adults and vice versa. So that you can better unlock this type of information regardless of the age of the secret-keeper, it's important to have a clear understanding of the many roles that secrets play during the various stages of people's lives.

Childhood Secrets

While childhood development is an ongoing process, there are two very important developmental stages in our younger lives that are worthy of examining with respect to secrecy. The first stage occurs before the child reaches twelve years of age and has two milestones within it. The second stage occurs during adolescence. Both these stages assist 'individualisation' of the child. This is when children start to establish a boundary between themselves and others; they start to develop into their own person; a more independent individual.

The first milestone in the first stage occurs quite young and is usually completed by the time the child reaches three to five years of age.[14] Being able to understand, and to a limited degree keep a secret, demonstrates that a child has reached that stage.[15] Certainly by the time children reach the age of five years, they have a firm understanding of secrecy.[16] By this stage they start to learn that they can possess knowledge that another person does not have and can therefore manipulate the other person's mind or knowledge of facts.[17] They learn to lie and they learn to keep secrets.

At this early stage though, children really are not very good at either. Not many four year olds can maintain a lie or effectively keep a secret from their parents for very long. Before we start to point the finger and think all children are 'lying little secret-keepers,' we should remember that this is a developmental milestone that we all transitioned through and which set us on our way towards developing into our own person.

So what kinds of secrets would such young children keep and why? A study of 180 schoolchildren from three different grades (grades three, five and seven) was designed to provide a picture of how children and their secret-keeping changes as they develop in early childhood.[18] The study showed that as children age they are more inclined to start keeping secrets to avoid shame and punishment, whereas younger children are more inclined to keep secrets about possessions. This shows that children develop social awareness and realize the consequences on relationships if secret information were revealed. Put simply, younger children are more focused on owning objects and possessions and will keep secrets to gain and protect them. This can be seen when younger children have difficulty or complain (usually loudly!) about sharing their toys or possessions with other children.

As children reach the ages of nine to twelve years, they usually have developed a firm understanding of society's expectations and that of other people (primarily their parents and friends). As such, they will keep secret information that may cause them to be viewed as unacceptable, or that will cause them embarrassment or result in punishment. During these years, they will on most occasions have friends of the same sex. These are usually the dominant social relationships for children of this age. Often the 'other' sex is not liked, may be despised and sometimes actively teased by the respective cohort, e.g. 'You have girl germs' or 'Boys smell,' etc.

In what seems like a cruel twist of fate, around this time most will start to harbor a curiosity and even develop crushes on one of the 'enemy gender'. They may even have a 'secret' relationship such as passing written notes, emails or conversations after school (of course). However, this information is kept secret out of fear of embarrassment or being judged unacceptable by friends; the child has now developed a social awareness of what information needs to be kept secret to maintain their relationships. Some parents may be allowed access to this secret information by the child and may also be asked for advice, but this is not always the case; out of the fear of embarrassment or anticipated judgement or punishment. Predominantly though it must be kept secret from friends and others.

Discovered childhood crushes and relationships with the other gender can be quickly ended by a teasing call across the school yard: 'Geoffrey's got a girlfriend' or 'Kerry and Sue are getting married.' This will usually result in a total denial by the children involved and the end of the relationship (sadly) sometimes follows these sorts of taunts. The secret has been revealed and the embarrassment and social unacceptability is simply too much.

In summary, there is a significant developmental point marked by the ability to understand and to keep secrets, usually occurring between the ages of three to five years. Secrets commencing around this age are predominantly focused upon gaining and protecting possessions, but there is little awareness of the social consequences if the secret is revealed. During the years following this, children's secrets change focus and become more centred on social expectation and relationships; they hide information or behavior that may be viewed as unacceptable or embarrassing, or result in their being punished.

Adolescent Secrets

The second stage of 'individualisation' occurs during adolescence when the child is breaking away from the bonds of childhood and approaching adulthood.[19] During this stage of life they become less dependent upon their parents and start to rely more upon friends and social networks for support. This is not to say that parents become unimportant, but adolescents become more emotionally independent. It is during these teenage years that they realize their parents are not all-knowing and they challenge that—ask anyone who has had teenagers, they will agree wholeheartedly! They are now also increasingly capable and willing to keep secrets from their parents as a way of staking their claim to emotional independence.

They also become quite proficient at lying and hiding information, not just from parents, but from others.[20] They learn to manipulate information to suit their purpose. They reveal some information, they conceal other information and they may also fabricate information to manipulate the way they are seen or perceived by others. A review of a teenager's Facebook account will clearly demonstrate this for you. Only the information (including photos) they want to shape others' perceptions is revealed through social networking sites; the rest is kept secret.

Now we can point our fingers at the *lying little secret keepers!* Or should we? Could this also be an indicator of what adults also do? Most (honest) adults would agree that they have, on occasion, kept some information secret and released other information to manipulate the way others see them. This may be during a first date, a job interview, at a party, a conference, with other parents and even with siblings—it's a normal and understandable human practice.

While it may be a necessary and natural part of development for adolescents to keep secrets from parents, is this healthy and should it be encouraged? An extensive study was conducted on the advantages and disadvantages of keeping secrets from parents on almost 1200 young adolescents.[21] These results brought into stark reality the danger and harm that can result when secrets, perhaps too many, are kept from parents. This study found that adolescent secret-keeping (from parents) was associated with psychological disadvantages leading to low self-esteem, depressive moods and increased levels of stress. Additionally, it increased levels of aggression and delinquency.

For teenagers, the psychological burden of carrying serious or too many secrets can take its toll both mentally and physically. While secret-keeping may assist in developing emotional independence, this independence may be established too early during adolescence, resulting in the child dealing with 'real world' adult-type relationships and problems in the absence of adult support and advice. This can be damaging for the teenager, who may increasingly become isolated as a direct consequence. For parents, these risk factors clearly demonstrate the worth of being able to access some of the secret information held by your teenage child. The elicitation skills taught in this book should assist you in gaining that access during conversations with your child without it appearing intrusive.

Adult Secrets

So far we have had an insight into the way secrets play a part in our lives as we develop. We have seen that during childhood and adolescence, secrecy is a normal part of developing. However, we have also seen that it can have a burdensome and negative impact upon both young children and adolescents. Fortunately, as we arrive at adulthood, we are more fully developed and are far more competent and resilient to the negative impacts of secrets—right? Wrong! What is revealed is that very similar detrimental consequences continue from adolescence into adulthood.

So what do adults keep secret? A variety of studies have been conducted to ascertain if there is a particular subject or applicable theme to adult secrets. Most research has determined that sex-related secrets are the dominant topic, followed by failure-related secrets including information that may portray or reveal a mental illness.[22] Sex-related does not only include events directly in relation to the act of sex itself, but also includes related activities such as sexual fantasies, perceived or real sexual inadequacies, sexual diseases, illegitimacy and abortion. Some significant examples of sex-related secrets that were volunteered during research include:

- 'I've been with my partner for 14 years and we've got kids. I've never told her I'm a cross dresser.'
- 'I am a married woman having an inappropriate (although sexless) relationship with a Roman Catholic priest.'[23]

- 'I have been happily married for 12 years—I had a one-night stand a few years ago. I regret it but it's a secret and a shame I have to carry for the rest of my life.'

Failure-related secrets include a self-observation of failure in respect to various areas including financial, spiritual, physical, social and intellectual matters.[24] Recent research was conducted into failure-related secrets in respect to smoking during pregnancy. In this study, 34% of women surveyed who stated they were not actively smoking (while pregnant) had their failure-related secret revealed during urine analysis.[25] These women attempted to keep this information secret due to embarrassment and/or the way others may adversely view them should their secret (smoking during pregnancy) be revealed. Other examples of reported failure-related secrets include:

- 'My family thinks I go to church regularly, but I haven't been for over a year.'

- 'I drive an expensive car and I have trendy clothes—I look successful, but my credit card debt is through the roof. Really I'm a financial failure, but no one knows, except my bank.'

- 'I'm in a senior management position and I supervise many people who have degrees and are more educated than me—they all assume I have a degree (or two), but I didn't even finish high school.'

'Masking' is also an often reported secret by adults. Masking relates to a person masking the truth to keep it secret by wearing a false facade. Reported examples of masking in adults include:

- 'I am a shy person but I put on an act so no one will know.'

- 'I'm highly unstable and insecure, but I hide this well and people come to me with their own problems expecting me to help because they consider me solid. I don't feel competent to aid them and yet to tell them this would lower my mask and perhaps scare them away permanently.'[26]

- 'I suffer from deep depression, but I put on a happy face at work, I make jokes and probably over compensate to hide how I feel. No one knows how I really feel.'

It is clear that keeping secrets is a normal part of human development, though the focus of our secrets changes as we travel through our lives. Keeping serious or too many secrets can be mentally burdensome and detrimental for young children, adolescents and also adults. In future you may be in a position to use elicitation skills to assist someone who is hiding significant and detrimental information.

Family Secrets

In this section, we examine family secrets and their effect on families. It may be expected that communication with respect to secrets within families would vary depending upon a family's configuration, i.e. traditional (mother and father), single parents and blended families (adoptive, remarried, etc.). However, research has shown that regardless of the family configuration they are all similar in respect to the number of perceived secrets, the topics of secrets and the function or aim of secrets within a family.[27] Some research results indicate that as high as 99% of family members keep at least one secret from one or more members of their family.[28] This form of secret-keeping is in fact very common—almost all of us don't share everything with family members; primarily for privacy, acceptance and independence.

Most families have shared jokes and family stories that are kept solely within the family; this helps strengthen family identity and closeness.[29] These are regular family matters and may also include unpleasant subject areas such as not being able to afford to go on holiday or one parent losing their job, or a grandparent passing away. These are not labelled a 'family secret,' nor are matters that are discussed between parents that occur out of the hearing of the children as part of normal parenting. This type of secrecy is normal within ordinary families.

So what is a 'family secret'? The type of secret referred to as a 'family secret' goes beyond the everyday situations. Examples that may be treated by a family as a 'family secret' include:

- A parent being addicted to prescription medication, alcohol or illegal drugs

- A tragic incident

- A mental disability or condition

- Abortion

- Adoption

- Incest

- HIV/AIDs

- Same sex relationships
- Paedophilia
- Eating disorders
- Child or spousal abuse

A family secret is a profound secret that psychologically binds one or more family members to never speak of the matter external to, and sometimes also within, the family home. Different families treat the same incident or event information differently; one with open communication and with external support, others by attempting to bury the information as a family secret. Sometimes family secrets are only known by some of the family members and other members are isolated and left out of the information loop.

Some families overtly make strict rules about non-disclosure of family secrets and others simply abide through a sense of loyalty or guilt that disclosure would add shame and additional problems for the family. Either way, whether implied or declared, these rules can prevent family members from seeking help and support and also inhibit medical, social, legal or law enforcement professionals from intervening. Elicitation conducted correctly by family members, a relative or a professional can assist the affected persons to talk about the hidden information and assist in managing a family secret.

How family secrets turn toxic

This reported case provides an indication of just how binding a family secret can be and demonstrates that such a secret may be detrimental to the next generation if not managed correctly.[30]

A family had two sons of similar age, John and Peter (names changed). John developed in a very normal way. Peter was gay and developed a perverse sexual interest in young boys when he reached adolescence.[31] Between the age of 15 and 18, Peter interfered with several young boys and this resulted in complaints being made to his parents on more than one occasion. For reasons unknown, these matters were not pursued by the police and no action was taken. John's father (a prominent lawyer) and his mother never discussed these complaints with the authorities or within the family. While John was well aware of these incidents and felt what Peter had done was wrong, he also felt a strong obligation to treat it as a secret—in line with the way his parents were dealing with the situation. John felt there was an 'unspoken binding family expectation' that no one would talk of Peter's 'condition'.

Years later, John married and had a son of his own. Such is the nature of family secrets; John kept his brother's paedophilia from his new wife. On several occasions, John and his wife allowed Peter to care for their son when they were away. Inevitably, John's son was molested by Peter and the incident was discovered. John then confided the family secret (that Peter was a paedophile) to his wife, who was understandably shocked and infuriated that she had been denied such critical information needed to protect their son. The marriage ended shortly after that incident.

This example demonstrates how the most abhorrent of family secrets can create a secrecy bond of considerable strength, extending past the trust of a marriage and even to the point of endangering the secret-keeper's own child. Family secrets can be nasty, damaging secrets and they can place a particular burden on children within those families who either carry the secret and are forbidden from talking about it (as occurred in John's case), or are isolated from other members within the family by not knowing the secret.

Correctly applied elicitation techniques shown in *Parts Three* and *Four* can assist greatly with managing those who are locked into living in isolation with a burdensome family secret.

Secrets in the Workplace

In this section we'll focus on areas of secrecy in the workplace. First, why businesses and management keep secrets and, secondly, why clients/patients keep secrets from people trying to help them.

Understanding why a client or patient may keep a secret from you when your whole focus is representing or supporting them will assist you to better apply elicitation tactics to unlock this information, so you will in turn provide them a better service. Similarly, if you are suspicious of what your management tells you, understanding why they may keep secrets from you will assist you in unlocking that information, which may better protect your interests and even your job!

Business and Management Secrets

Twenty-first century business is built on highly sensitive information such as advancements in technology, software and sophisticated design and innovation. A competitive edge is often quickly found by learning a competitor's hidden information. So logically, businesses seek to protect information such as customer lists, business plans, methods of operations and employee information which to another company could be commercially invaluable. In both the public and private sector there is big business in protecting secrets and in knowing the secrets of others.

Understandably it is illegal to steal information such as this. To protect against theft and illegal dissemination by employees, most companies have advanced internet protection measures, document tracking and email auditing capabilities to ensure any illegally accessed and disclosed information can be narrowed down to a particular employee. This is imperative as a company's most prized information is most often data based and can be stolen or given away with just a few mouse clicks.

To augment these measures, companies use additional strategies such as computer log-in security messages to act as a reminder to staff of the need to keep sensitive information within the company, enforcing the need-to-know principle and having employees sign non-disclosure agreements. Perhaps this is taking it too far? We know that if a person leaks confidential information, then a civil damages lawsuit can be successful and awarded against that person. However, in many cases the damages awarded pale into insignificance if a company's secret is published, as once this occurs, legally, it can never be 'secret' again and others may use this information freely. When this occurs a company may never recover that lost competitive edge.

Some advanced companies teach their staff basic counter-elicitation skills which enable employees to detect when they are being surreptitiously targeted by elicitation. This is becoming more and more necessary as companies are increasingly turning to elicitation to learn the sensitive information of others. The reason this is the case is that the theft of data and other sensitive commercial information via technologies or by paying a competitor's employee may constitute a criminal offence. However, if a company were to use elicitation strategies that resulted in another company's employee voluntarily and verbally sharing sensitive information, this may simply be viewed as poor judgement on the part of that employee.[32]

There always remains at the very core of most business entities, a small trusted group of senior managers. This small 'inner circle' keeps the most sensitive and significant secrets of the organisation. If you are of a mind to need information about a company or organisation, it's members of this group you should target with elicitation techniques. Some may consider that members of such groups would be impervious to elicitation. However, as shown in *Part Two* under 'Casting Your Elicitation Line,' there are some strategies that senior management are particularly vulnerable to.

One of the most sensitive planning secrets held by an organization's 'information elite' has many terms such as, 'workforce re-engineering,' 'organizational or functional realignment,' 'efficiency review,' 'restructuring' and 'voluntary redundancy review' (sometimes followed by involuntary ones!). In most cases, regardless of the latest corporate buzz word for it, it spells possible job losses. These are not spur-of-the-moment processes and there will usually have been a lot of work conducted behind closed doors by the 'inner circle' group for a number of weeks, before those most affected by the changes are informed. Senior management do their best to keep this process a secret as long as possible.

There are various reasons for this. First, when members of a workplace learn there is a possibility that they may lose their job, they logically start looking for other places to work and it's usually the most talented employees who'll secure a job first, leaving the lower achievers at the company. Secondly, senior management sometimes consider it a possible corporate sabotage risk if the hidden plan to retrench staff is leaked. Disaffected staff, if they have the opportunity, may interfere with the proper running of the company or seek some type of retribution.

If a survey conducted in the United Kingdom is an indicator, those fears are well founded. That survey found that 88% of IT administrators stated they would steal company secrets, including CEO passwords, research and development plans and customer database information if they were made redundant.[33] So it is understandable that some senior managers are nervous about secret planned staffing cuts being leaked.

On a positive note, as these processes usually take some weeks before any announcement is made, it provides you with a good opportunity to use your new found skills to access this secret information to better protect yourself and your job. Forewarned is forearmed!

Elicitation in business, as with most undercover skills, exists in a grey area. As mentioned earlier, the purpose of this book is not to assist with criminal behavior nor is it to provide ethical guidance for people on when to use these secret-revealing skills; this is a matter for the reader and the many different circumstances where these skills may be applied. However, if it is critical to learn (legally) another company's sensitive information, then elicitation may be considered a viable enabling corporate option.

Clients Keeping Secrets

If you are a doctor, lawyer, psychologist, counsellor or other professional, you probably expect that you have your clients' trust and they would not keep secrets from you. After all, your job is focused upon helping them, correct? They know you are ethically, and in some cases legally, bound to keep their information secret, and you strive for open dialogue with clients, so you may best represent their interests or treat them. So, logically they wouldn't lie to you—right?

If you have read my book *Lie Catcher*, you would have already detected that many of your clients do lie and as such keep secrets from you. This is supported by several research studies. In one study it was revealed that almost 50% of long-term therapy clients kept secrets from their respective counsellors.[34] In a separate confidential study that guaranteed in writing to participants that the results would remain confidential, parents and teenagers consistently under-reported (kept secret) their drug use, which was later confirmed by hair sample analysis.[35] Keeping in mind the participants were provided a written guarantee about confidentiality, it begs the question, how honest are clients and patients in the absence of a written assurance?

Perhaps this result was so high because the subject involved criminal behavior? However, earlier in the book we discussed a similar result where 34% of women surveyed stated they were not actively smoking while pregnant had their secret (they had actually been smoking) revealed during urine analysis.[36] This indicates that clients/patients don't only keep information secret when it is related to criminal activity. So why do clients keep secrets from those trying to assist them?

Anita Kelly researched a wide variety of medical clients who kept secrets from their therapist. She found that over half were either afraid to express feelings, were too embarrassed or ashamed to reveal the secret or didn't want the therapist to know of the lack of progress being made.[37] There is relevance in these findings when you consider that, despite a qualified professional trying to have an open and honest relationship, there exists a power differential. This can make some clients feel that they will somehow be morally or ethically judged by the professional.

An example of this is where a defence lawyer's client keeps secret a criminal conviction to appear a more 'worthy' person or to avoid shame or embarrassment. Similarly, 13% of patients who smoke keep this a secret from their doctor.[38] Of those who do keep their smoking a secret, two-thirds do so to avoid being judged and/or lectured about their habit. In both cases the clients knew that their information would be treated confidentially and the secret information was not illegal. Importantly, in both cases the client would have been better supported had they been honest, but they chose to keep the information secret.

How can a professional help, treat, support or otherwise represent a client's interests if secrets are kept from them? The simple answer is that they can't. If you are in such a position and you are attempting to uncover hidden information from a client or patient, it is imperative to explicitly inform the person that the information is privileged and cannot legally be divulged, and additionally, that the person won't be judged or lectured about any aspect of the information they provide, just supported or treated. This should alleviate the number one reason why clients and patients hide information. In addition to this, using the elicitation strategies in *Parts Three* and *Four* will assist the client/patient to reveal all their hidden information and be better supported by doing so.

The Effect and Influence of Secrets

Secret Attractions, Secret Relationships and White Bears

One of the reasons I want to discuss this aspect of hidden information is that attraction, born from secret relationships, can be used as an important component of the elicitation lines discussed later in the book. An insight into this phenomenon can assist with extreme rapid rapport building with new people and enhance existing personal and professional relationships.

Before we discuss this, though, I think it's helpful to have an understanding of what a secret relationship is, and is not. A secret relationship may include secrets *within* a relationship, but also secrets *of* a relationship; a relationship that is kept secret from others. An example is where a senior manager and his/her personal assistant have an affair. Overtly, in front of all in the workplace their relationship is professional and platonic. However, covertly they are having a sexual relationship. Staff in the office have no knowledge of the relationship. In this situation, staff are not simply unaware through ignorance. This secret relationship is *deliberately* engineered to keep it hidden from others. It's a relationship that, if revealed, would be harmful, hurtful or offensive to others, or detrimental to one or both parties.

Similarly, a secret relationship may exist between two employees of competing companies. Due to their friendship, they may share inside information with each other about their respective companies. Neither company would approve of this, so both employees keep the relationship hidden.

A secret relationship may also be a 'one way' relationship, such as a secret crush on another person. This may include a person's innocent secret affection for or fantasy about an unsuspecting other (such as film stars, or other people with whom they work or interact with), but it may also relate to more sinister stalking-type relationships.

The strongest indicator of a secret relationship is where one or both within the relationship would lie to protect the very existence of it. We'll use this simple description for the purposes of this book: 'A secret relationship occurs between two people when one or both of them keep the relationship itself or secret information shared within it, secret from others.'

While the dynamics and effect of secrecy in relationships is a complex area of psychology, and there is a lot yet to be learned in this area, it is clear from the research that secrecy enhances attraction. Put simply, those involved in secret relationships have amplified and sometimes disproportionate feelings of attraction.

This was demonstrated in a study which had two groups of people undertake surveillance of a person of the opposite gender, following the person continuously.[39] One group was told they didn't need to keep the surveillance secret as the person being followed knew about the activity. The other group was told to keep the surveillance covert, as the person being followed was unaware of the surveillance. The results of this study showed that those who followed the person in secret became more attracted to the person than those who overtly conducted surveillance.

This phenomenon has also occurred in real life law enforcement surveillance operations. There was an investigation into an organised crime group in Australia, who were suspected of importing cocaine, LSD and pseudoephedrine. The crime group were sophisticated and very tenacious at hiding their activities; as such, an extended surveillance operation which lasted over 12 months targeted the group.

During that phase of the investigation, covert surveillance operatives legally intercepted conversations and telephone calls, followed, photographed and filmed the primary suspects. During full-time surveillance operations such as this, the surveillance operatives effectively become voyeurs of almost every aspect of the suspects' lives. During this particular operation, this psychologically affected one operative who became obsessed with and attracted to one of the crime syndicate members. This led to the operative having a physical relationship with the suspect. This was clearly highly inappropriate and dangerous, but it is a good demonstration of the immense and influential magnetism that can manifest in a secret relationship.

Secret relationships don't always include physical attraction. It may be confined to emotional and psychological attraction to another person. As we'll see later, secrets are most often told to people a secret-keeper 'likes'. We can use the nature of secret relationships to increase our attractiveness to others and cause them to 'like' us. These strategies work in a dating scene, a marriage, at work and, importantly, when eliciting hidden information.

For example, a person may wish to know some inside information about a competing company. As such the person approaches an employee of that company. At some stage during their conversation, he falsely states, 'Just between you and I, our sales are down by 34%. It's all being kept quiet but I think we may be in real trouble if things don't change. Please don't tell anyone I told you though. I suppose your company is doing well?' If the person then responds with some similar 'inside' information there is a secret relationship being created—one that, if asked, either party would deny existed.

Research shows that the content and nature of the information or activity is of little consequence; it is more the activity of sharing secrecy more so than the secret itself that breeds intimacy.[40] Daniel Wenger, who has undertaken considerable research into secret relationships, sums up attraction in secret relationships best: 'Secrecy appears to form a social bond of considerable strength, one that may be the basis for an individual's attraction to and pre-occupation with a partner.'[41] It's clear that secret relationships create a closeness between strangers that would not have blossomed if secrecy were not an ingredient of the relationship. However, obsession may also be a by-product of secret relationships.

To access a person's secret we may seek to deliberately use the nature of secret relationships to our advantage, by sharing a secret to increase how much a secret-keeper likes us and to amplify the compulsion to share their own secret. However, we need to moderate this as we don't want to become the object of the secret-keeper's obsession. For a quick demonstration why, watch the movie *Fatal Attraction*!

Some Russian folklore may assist in understanding the strange obsessive by-product of secret relationships. The Russian story tells of a man who instructs his younger brother to sit in a corner of the room and to not think about white bears.[42] The harder the brother tries to suppress the thoughts of white bears, the more he thinks about them. This escalates to the point where there is little he can do apart from thinking about whites bears.

Applying the same concept but in a different context, this 'white bear' phenomenon is something I am vulnerable to and can relate to—perhaps you can too. In quiet, controlled situations such as during speeches, in elevators, at lectures or as a child at school assemblies someone whispering to me, 'Don't laugh but ...' can spell the end of my composure. Before they even tell me the information, I'm already smiling. In fact, from that point I'm a lost cause, because the harder I try to not laugh the funnier it is! On more than one occasion I have had to excuse myself from supposedly 'adult situations' to go outside and release the laughter—even when I haven't heard all the information. The more I try not to laugh, the harder it is not to! This is the white bear theory in action.

Dr Daniel Wenger actually tested the 'white bear' theory.[43] As part of his laboratory research, he had subjects enter a room by themselves with a tape recorder to record everything that came into their mind during a five-minute period. Before each person entered the room, they were either told to think about white bears, or to *not* think about white bears. In the room was a bell, which the person was to ring each time the thought of white bears arose. The results showed that those who tried to suppress the white bear thoughts rang the bell more often than those who were free to think about them.

Interestingly in an elicitation context, when the roles were reversed and the group that had previously been told *not* to think about white bears were then permitted to—they rang the bell far more often than the first group who were initially told to think about white bears. Put another way, those who had first been told to suppress some information and were later told they were free to reveal it, continued to reveal the information they were first suppressing—more so than the group who were always free to reveal it!

What this means to us is that when we elicit information from a person who has deliberately hidden the information for some time, the secret information will flow more freely and rapidly than if it had not been a secret in the first place. In short, once the person reveals some hidden information to us, the person will then remain motivated to continue sharing hidden information.

We can use this to our advantage. We do this by making one of our aims, when eliciting information, to have the person share a secret, any secret, even a minor one. Once the person does this it's the commencement of a secret relationship and with a bit of nurturing, the small insignificant secret sharing will blossom into full disclosure.

Can Unlocking Secrets Result in Health Benefits?

Depending upon the nature of the secret and how much of a negative impact it may have on the secret-keeper (or someone they know), a person may share that information when the emotional hurt has faded to such a degree that it appears comfortable to do so. The person may share the information with a confidante, partner or friend, or it may never surface and remain buried in the secret-keeper's mind.

Regarding secret relationships, earlier we learned that in line with the 'white bear' tests, attempting to suppress information can lead to intrusive thoughts (unwanted thoughts invading the mind) and mental preoccupation by the secret-keeper about the secret person or incident. Considering the significant amount of mental energy required to maintain a secret and the possibility of intrusive and obsessive thought patterns, is it possible that when a significant secret is never shared it could actually make the secret-keeper mentally or physically sick?

Most people would expect there would be an increased stress level for people who harbor significant secrets over a long period of time. Alarmingly, there is some persuasive research which suggests the consequences can go well beyond that. One study of 344 college students who kept secret information they perceived would be viewed as negative by others showed a direct relationship to shyness, depression, anxiety and low self-esteem.[44] In another study, a group of children who had been hospitalized with symptoms of a psychotic disorder were found to have suffered the disorder due to the strain of keeping a 'family secret' hidden over an extended period.[45]

These are extreme examples and I'm not suggesting that keeping a secret will always have a significant negative consequence. However, these studies support most people's expectation that the mental strain of keeping secrets can adversely affect the state of mind of the secret-keeper.

The consequences can also extend beyond the psychological. An extensive controlled study of adult human services workers demonstrated that keeping secrets from others was not only directly linked with depression and anxiety, but also physical manifestations such as headaches and back pain.[46]

Another study conducted into the health of gay men produced surprising results and confirmed that keeping secrets can affect the physical health of people, not just their psychiatric wellbeing. This study compared the health of gay men who had openly disclosed their homosexuality against those who kept it a secret. After a five-year period, it was revealed that the latter group had a higher incidence of cancer and increased levels of infectious diseases such as pneumonia, bronchitis, sinusitis, and tuberculosis. According to Dr Steve Cole and other architects of this study, 'These effects could not be attributed to differences in age, ethnicity, socioeconomic status, repressive coping style, health-relevant behavioral patterns (e.g. drug use, exercise), anxiety, depression, or reporting biases (e.g. negative affectivity, social desirability).'[47] It wasn't the fact that they were gay that was making them sick, it was the fact that they kept it a secret!

Clearly, there is an abundance of research that demonstrates keeping a significant secret over a long period of time can take its toll on both the psychological and physical wellbeing of the secret-keeper.

So if keeping secrets can make you sick, can it be 'healing' to divulge them? In short, yes. In one study, a longer survival period of breast cancer patients was recorded in those who shared their secrets.[48] This was not an isolated finding; other credible studies have found similar beneficial results.

Dr James Pennebaker has studied this aspect of secrets for over two decades and has produced some very interesting and beneficial results.[49] Dr Pennebaker investigated why secret-keepers were more prone to medical problems, and if people shared information about a traumatic experience whether their health improved as a result. The results were quite amazing. It was shown in two different experiments that writing about a traumatic experience provided immediate health benefits to the secret-keeper.

The first study of university students (who always seem to be experimental fodder for scientists!) was assigned to four separate groups to write on four consecutive days, about one of the below:

- A trivial event, or

- Facts about a traumatic event, or

- Emotions surrounding a traumatic event, or

- Both facts and emotions surrounding a traumatic event.

In the six months subsequent to the writing tests, the students who wrote about 'both facts and emotions surrounding a traumatic event' made less health centre visits than all other group members.

In the second study (again on unsuspecting students) the participants were tested for their body's immune system response capability both before and after writing about either a trivial event or a traumatic personal event; again on four consecutive days. The students who wrote about a traumatic event showed a significantly higher immune system response (that's a good thing!) than those who wrote about trivial events. The results clearly showed a healthy response to writing about these events.[50]

People who write expressively and honestly about these types of events also have lower levels of anxiety and negative thought rumination. Even more surprising was the fact that these results and subsequent tests have verified that writing about a secret for 15 to 20 minutes on four consecutive days produces immediate health benefits—even if the notes are destroyed and not shown to another person!

It may be the case that you are attempting to elicit hidden information from a person in order to better support or treat the person. If that person feels the secret is so embarrassing, abhorrent or distasteful that there is no one they can tell, it may be a sensible first step to undertake similar writing practices to Dr Pennebaker's research and then destroy their notes.[51] A person doing this would therefore not have to share the information with anyone else (they can simply write about it), but would gain a health benefit in doing so.

PART ONE KEY POINTS

To serve as a memory aid, below I have listed the key points from *Part One* for easy reference.

The Secret Nature of Secrets

- Secrets are an elusive and very complex psychological phenomena that are naturally a part of everyone's life; we all have secrets and it's natural that people want some information kept secret or told to just a very few.

- A secret is 'the intentional concealment of information from others'. 'Others' may include entities such as businesses, corporations, clubs and governments and also people such as partners, children, friends, work colleagues and complete strangers.

- The person who possesses secret information is termed a 'secret-keeper'.

- Those who are intentionally not provided secret information are called the 'secret-target,' as they are 'targeted' or disadvantaged by the secret.

- There are two types of secrets;

  - Self-focused, kept for the benefit of the secret-keeper.

  - Other-focused secrets kept for the benefit of another person or entity.

- Elicitation is the process of verbally acquiring hidden information from another person.

Childhood Secrets

- Research has shown that as children age they are more inclined to start keeping secrets to avoid shame and punishment, whereas younger children are more inclined to keep secrets about possessions. This shows that as children develop, their social awareness increases and they realize the consequences on relationships if the secret information were revealed.

- Younger children are more focused upon owning objects and possessions and will keep secrets to gain and protect them. Older children will keep secrets due to the adverse social consequences.

Adolescent Secrets

- Adolescent secret-keeping assists in developing emotional independence; however, if established too early during adolescence it results in the child dealing with *real world* adult-type relationships and problems in the absence of adult support and advice.

- Significant or too many secrets kept from parents by a teenager can lead to psychological disadvantages such as low self-esteem, depressive moods, increased levels of stress, aggression, delinquency, and can reduce their degree of self-control.

- Adolescents become skilled at manipulating information to suit their purpose; revealing some information, concealing other information; they may also fabricate information to engineer the way they are perceived by others.

Adult Secrets

- For adult secret-keepers, very similar detrimental consequences continue from adolescence into adulthood.

- Research has shown that sex-related secrets are the dominant adult secret topic, followed by failure-related secrets.

- Keeping serious secrets, or too many secrets, can be just as mentally burdensome and detrimental to adults as it is for children and adolescents.

Family Secrets

- Research has shown that regardless of the family configuration they are all similar in respect to the number of perceived secrets, the topics of secrets and the function or aim of secrets within a family.

- Family secrets go beyond the everyday situations where a family or some of its members want to keep some things private from each other or the outside world, or where parents keep information from their children as part of normal parenting.

- A family secret is a profound secret that psychologically binds one or more family members to never speak of the matter external to, and sometimes also within, the family home.

- Family secrets, regardless of the family's configuration, can be toxic and perpetuated from one generation to another if left untreated or unresolved. This can lead to a lifetime of difficulty in communication and relationships between those in the family who know the secret and those who don't.

Secrets in the Workplace

- All companies, corporations and businesses keep secrets to protect their interests. At the core of these entities exists a small select group that keeps the most sensitive and significant secrets of the organisation. If you want information about a company or organisation, its members of this group you should target with elicitation techniques.

- Some senior members and even CEOs are particularly vulnerable to some elicitation strategies.

- Often sensitive commercial information is better protected by secrecy than by using legal avenues such as trademark, intellectual property laws or patents. This is because company secrets can be protected indefinitely by secrets, whereas patents and other legal mechanisms usually have a statutory and finite life span.

- Regardless of how discrete and open a professional may try to be with clients, customers and patients, research has shown that many will still keep relevant information secret.

The Influence of Secrecy

- A secret relationship occurs between two people when one or both of them keep the relationship itself, or secret information shared within it, secret from others. This also includes a 'one way' secret relationship, such as a secret crush on another who is unaware of the crush.

- Secrecy forms a social bond of considerable strength, one that may be the basis for an individual's attraction to and pre-occupation with the partner in a secret relationship.

- One of our aims when eliciting information is to have the person share a secret, any secret, even a minor one. Once this occurs the person will have a lower resilience to withhold hidden information from us.

- There is an abundance of research that demonstrates keeping a significant secret over a long period of time can take its toll on both the psychological and physical wellbeing of the secret-keeper.

- According to Dr James Pennebaker, writing about the facts and emotions surrounding a secret for 15 to 20 minutes on four consecutive days produces immediate health benefits.

Part Two:

Science in the Art of Unlocking Secrets

If you have completed reading *Part One* you will now have a robust understanding of why people keep secrets. This part will provide you with some essential knowledge on how to unlock those secrets, before moving on to the practical aspects of accessing hidden information in *Parts Three* and *Four*.

The adage 'knowledge is power' is usually true, but power is usually reduced when the information is widely shared. Secret knowledge, however, remains powerful and can provide a significant advantage for the secret-keeper. Conversely, the power of such knowledge may be destructive for the secret-keeper, as is the case with some family secrets (discussed in *Part One*) or in the case of a child keeping secrets about being abused or bullied. In these latter cases, sharing the secret information (with a parent, teacher or counsellor) will reduce the powerful impact and dilute the negative influence of the secret information.

As a parent, teacher or counsellor, being able to access the harmful secrets of a troubled child can provide a greater level of understanding and allow better support for the child. In business, it can be a major advantage to know the hidden information of other companies, competitors and even colleagues. For senior managers, HR executives and workplace interviewers, being able to access hidden information can provide an insight into the *real* situation, add significant value to decision-making and aid improved workplace management.

For police and other law enforcement professionals, being able to have a person of interest volunteer information in the absence of coercion of any sort can greatly enhance the accuracy and efficacy of an investigation and also the reliability and quality of evidence. In our personal lives, some associates, friends and even our intimate partners may keep information hidden that you may need to know to better protect yourself or to better know and understand that person.

In all these cases, it is an advantage to know what is being hidden from us. Being the target of someone's secrecy can place you at a disadvantage or leave you vulnerable. Despite this, on occasion others aim to keep information to themselves or to share it with some—but not you. Fortunately, there are some scientific aspects of secret-keeping and some clever interpersonal techniques that we can utilize to uncover that hidden information; the process is called elicitation.

What is Elicitation?

'Elicitation' is both a term and a tactic used extensively by government intelligence agencies, covert operatives and undercover agents to describe the subtle verbal extraction of information from persons of interest. Put simply, elicitation is a conversation with a learning agenda. Secret agents and spies who use skilful elicitation techniques are able to learn a great deal from the person of interest who, if questioned directly, would refuse to provide that information.

Some may think that type of activity only occurs in the world of espionage and has no relevance to our daily lives. I don't believe that is the case; we are the victims of elicitation every day. Individuals and companies are attempting to extract information from us constantly. Perhaps I'm being thoroughly paranoid? I don't think so . . .

Pause and ask yourself if you have ever registered on an internet site by providing some of your information so you may comment, blog, receive special deals or vouchers, make purchases, join the discussion forum or gain access to the subscriber's area. Have you ever filled out a quick questionnaire that offers the chance of a prize, or left your business card in a bowl on the counter of a shop that offers a monthly prize to one business card holder? Innocent and non-threatening enough, but our information is being elicited from us, even if we mask our real identity.

Consider how many 'rewards cards' you may have and the number of 'customer loyalty programs you participate in. For example, cards used when travelling (frequent flyers and electronic public transportation cards), places you stay (hotel rewards programs), making purchases using both your 'earn points' and credit cards, and loyalty cards for fuel, food, groceries, coffee, clothing, etc. These all gain you points, gifts or discounts, but they are also a very effective way for companies to 'elicit' information from you, ranging from your personal details (when you first join) to your purchasing, eating, travel and banking habits and preferences. Even the type of reward you select or how you spend your reward/gift provides vital marketing information for the collecting company. Our participation and use of reward cards and customer loyalty programs have been so normalized in our lives that we simply accept it as a part of 21st century living and we unsuspectingly provide constantly updated information to others who use it for their commercial benefit.

If these companies wrote to us and asked us to provide all our purchasing and travel information and to keep them updated periodically—in the absence of a financial reward or gift—most of us would simply refuse to share such an array of information. However, we happily participate by using these cards and we are not alone. This type of 'elicitation line' successfully works on millions of people around the world by promising a benefit and *very* subtly disguising that a vast amount of our personal information is being electronically taken from us—this is corporate elicitation, and it works.

These programs use the 'elicitation line' of financial incentive or advantage and it works on most people. ('Elicitation lines' are discussed in detail in *Part Three*.) The 'elicitation line' you will use to provide as an incentive for the secret-keeper to share information will vary depending on the circumstances and the person, but unlike corporations and spy agencies you won't ever have to bribe the person with money!

In our working lives, we attend meetings, business conferences, trade shows and presentations. We have all learned the benefits of 'networking,' which is simply the process of meeting useful contacts for our own, or mutual benefit. In all these situations, people make conversation with each other and remember interesting or useful information. As part of business or personal networking, people are deliberately engaged in conversation with the view to creating useful contacts. You may have noticed a person who is a very effective networker and has developed a diverse array of useful contacts and seems to have an insight into a lot that's going on. That person has either naturally or purposefully learned elicitation skills. I think it is fair to say that elicitation is part of our everyday lives, and those most effective at it, gain the most advantage and best protection as a result of those skills.

A secret-keeper (business competitor, deceptive client, criminal suspect, staff member, management executive, lying child or student) is likely to refuse to answer our direct and obvious questions about information that is hidden from us. Alternatively, a secret-keeper may not be deliberately hiding the information— it may psychologically be too difficult to tell you the secret information, or to even recall it accurately, e.g. they may be a victim of crime, child or spousal abuse. In both cases the information needs to be elicited from the person. We just need to use different tactics and 'elicitation lines' to successfully do this. Elicitation is *not* about intimidation or coercing information from a person, nor is it about causing the person to fabricate information; it's about uncovering the truth, that's wrapped up in a secret form.

If we elicit the information correctly, it will be an enjoyable conversation for both the secret-keeper and the secret-target (that's you). I'm sure at some stage you have met a person who seems difficult to connect with. The person isn't deliberately being difficult, it's just that you seem to be on a different wavelength and communication is difficult, jokes fall flat or the person just doesn't get you. Similarly, perhaps you've met with an overly eager or inexperienced salesperson who seems to be doing all the talking, or you may have been on the phone to a company that seems more interested in validating your identity and selling you something than really listening to what you have to say. These are good examples of exactly the way we *don't* want the secret-keeper to feel about their interaction with you.

At some stage you may have met with a person who you thoroughly enjoyed talking with, and felt that you could talk to them all day. Some describe these people as 'good listeners'. While the person may not have had a hidden agenda of eliciting information from you, they have naturally developed elicitation skills. As a result, you felt very comfortable conversing and may have even shared more detailed information than you would normally and would like to talk with the person again as you enjoyed the person's company. That is exactly the way we *do* want secret-keepers to feel about their interaction with you.

Elicitation in Action

On one occasion an agency was investigating a senior member of an outlaw motorcycle gang. Investigators became concerned because the person's bank accounts and phone had simply stopped being used on the same date. Considering his passport had not been used, he should have been in the country and been able to be located using surveillance operatives. However, there was suddenly no trace of the person, anywhere. There are a number of reasons why all traces of a person's activities can cease on a particular date. These include being spooked by law enforcement interest and as a result the person starts hiding, the person has left the country using a false passport or has been killed. None of these are favorable outcomes to investigators.

The person had a 'relatively' law abiding non-bikie brother who he was close to. It was ascertained the brother would most likely know the suspect's whereabouts. In this situation, the brother was the secret-keeper. If I were to simply approach the brother and ask direct questions to find out where the suspect was or what had happened, his response would not have been favourable. However, using the READ Model of Elicitation model (discussed later), I approached the brother at his local hotel and spent some time engaging him in conversation about a number of topics. During one of our conversations, he informed me that his brother was on a camping, shooting and fishing trip in an isolated part of Australia.

As this was a place where there were no banks or mobile phone reception, it explained the person's apparent disappearance. After a suitable time I left the hotel. The brother had clearly enjoyed the conversation and would have welcomed me back had I returned at some stage in the future. When elicitation is conducted correctly, the information from the secret-keeper flows so naturally and so fluidly that the person feels relaxed and comfortable and doesn't even question why they are sharing so much information with you. That was the case with the bikie's brother.

From a business perspective some people may ask why use elicitation? Isn't it enough to simply research all the competitor information from corporate publications and reports on the internet and not have to talk to anyone? A businessperson may spend many hours researching a competitor's marketing and business strategies to better compete against a particular company. However, the problem even with in-depth research of this nature is that print is only accurate on the day it's printed, things change constantly, websites aren't updated regularly and businesses only release the information they want others to know.

On the other hand, humans remain up to date and can provide insight into the human and commercial dynamics of a competitor including concepts and future strategies. It's an important insight that only a person can provide. In business, skilfully executed elicitation will produce accurate and reliable information that others, who rely on paper and electronic based research, simply cannot learn.

To achieve this we can follow the READ Model of Elicitation (explained in *Part Four*) to guide us through the process. However, before we move on to that it's helpful to understand the two categories of elicitation—direct elicitation and indirect elicitation—as there are different elicitation tools applicable to each category.

Direct Elicitation

Direct elicitation can simply be described as an elicitation process where the secret-keeper is aware that you are attempting to learn their hidden information. This can occur in more structured settings, such as an interview-like situation. However, it may also be conducted in a less structured environment; for example, by a parent who is wanting to find out information from their teenager about what they have done or are planning to do without the process seeming like an interrogation.

Direct elicitation is, as the name subjects, a direct approach with obvious questions being asked of the secret-keeper. However, this doesn't mean that just the conventional question and answer process takes place. We need to apply direct elicitation techniques beyond this to improve our chance of success. In the absence of these techniques, the hidden information would most likely remain so—as the person can simply refuse to answer, or may have difficulty recalling the required information.

Examples of Direct Elicitation

Workplace interviews including:

- Investigation of complaints, accidents or other incidents
- Performance feedback sessions
- Selection panel interviews
- Personnel vetting interviews
- Past employment history checking and referee verification
- Parents or teachers asking children (who perhaps don't want to implicate their friend/s) about an incident the child witnessed, or possibly to reveal their own misbehavior.
- Welfare situations where parents, teachers, counsellors or medical professionals ask about hidden traumatic information, such as being a victim of crime, road accidents, bullying, grief counselling, etc.
- Medical practitioners asking patients questions about information the patient may not want to volunteer freely, such as illegal drug use, smoking, hidden eating disorders, excessive drinking, etc.

- Police officers, investigators and security personnel questioning a suspect, informant or witness

As you can see, direct elicitation is used in any situation where the person has hidden information and is aware you are seeking that information.

Direct Elicitation Techniques

Most effective elicitation techniques can be applied to both direct and indirect elicitation situations. However, there are some techniques that are specifically very effective when you are in a position of power and are asking direct questions to access the information you require. Direct elicitation techniques include:

- **Avoiding a stalemate**: Asking questions with 'wriggle room' so the person doesn't back themself into a corner.
- **Dissolving authority barriers and demonstrating emotional empathy:** To quickly build rapport with the person and have them open up to you.
- **Asking open-ended questions**: So the person cannot shut the conversation down with a simple 'yes' or 'no' answer.
- **Using silence**: To cause the person to speak.

These four techniques work very effectively with the READ Model of Elicitation and are further explained below together with some examples.

Avoiding Stalemate—Asking Questions with Wriggle Room

In an interview-type situation, there is a tendency to ask a direct question to get to the bottom of the matter. However, often such an approach is simply met with a refusal or a stubborn denial and it can extinguish the person's motivation to communicate. This unproductively positions the two people in opposing corners creating a stalemate.

Stalemates

Parent/teacher: 'Tell me who threw the ball through the window?'
Child/student (secret-keeper): 'I don't know.'

Workplace accident investigator: 'Did you leave the floor wet?'
Suspect (secret-keeper): 'No.'

Shop assistant (clothing being returned): 'Have you worn this item?'
Purchaser (secret-keeper): 'No.'

In these situations, the secret-keepers are now locked into their story and they can't deviate from this or it will reveal that they have lied, causing them embarrassment, loss of face, ridicule, or even facing a penalty or punishment. So a conversational stalemate is reached. When two people are firmly locked in opposing corners, there is a total communications breakdown and it can be very difficult to overcome.

Nothing will lock a secret-keeper's information more securely than if you ask a question that forces the person to blatantly lie. This locks them into a 'denial corner'. Once in that corner, they cannot tell the truth without exposing themselves as having lied.

Once a secret-keeper is committed to an outright denial, it takes a lot of psychological pressure before the person will capitulate and come clean with the truth.

We don't want to enter into a battle with the person's ego or pride, so the trick here is to strike before they lie themselves into the corner. We do this by asking questions with 'wriggle room' so the person may tell at least a half-truth. This is usually wrapped up in a vague answer rather than an outright lie or denial. It's fine if the person lies about one aspect of the matter but gives you some truthful information. You can then work on the truthful aspect to access the whole truth later in the conversation, without the secret-keeper feeling like s/he have been exposed as a liar.

Allowing for wriggle room

Using the same scenarios as in the examples above, but rephrasing the questions to allow wriggle room.

Parent/teacher: 'Do you think you could help me find out who threw the ball through the window?' *(Even if this is met with a vague denial, the child hasn't blatantly denied any knowledge, so later in the conversation, if the child does give some information, it doesn't come at the cost of being seen as a liar—therefore it is more likely the child will be forthcoming.)*

Child/student: 'I don't think I can.' *(This is a much better response than an outright 'no,' so the parent/teacher can then work with the child to elicit what actually happened.)*

Workplace accident investigator: 'Have you received training on how to clean up safely in the workplace?' *(This allows the person a 'loop hole' that may excuse them to some degree for leaving the floor wet. It doesn't change the facts of the incident being investigated, but a question such as this is more likely to lead to a confession later in the conversation.)*

Suspect: 'Well, I've cleaned up plenty of times, but I've never actually been trained.'

Shop assistant (clothing being returned): 'This appears to have been worn. Do you think someone wore it before you bought it?'

Purchaser: 'It's possible; maybe that did happen.' *(This provides a loop hole for the purchaser and allows some wriggle room in the answer. At this point the purchaser has admitted the clothing has been worn—that's a crucial gain. The next step is to ask how could it be that the 'worn condition' of the clothing wasn't picked up at point of sale by the purchaser or the checkout assistant; as the questions slowly close the loop hole towards an admission.)*

A conversational stalemate is the greatest enemy of uncovering hidden information; it simply stalls the flow of all information. This is the worst situation and should be avoided by asking questions with 'wriggle room,' that frees the flow of both true and untrue information.

Any conversation, even one laced with lies, is better than an outright denial. The solution is to ask questions with wriggle room; allowing the secret-keeper to tell both some truth and some lies—*before* they can make a total denial.

Dissolve Authoritative Barriers and Demonstrate Emotional Empathy

In the previous list of direct elicitation examples, you may have noticed that the person seeking the hidden information is usually (not always) in a position of authority, by position, expertise or profession, over the secret-keeper. If you are in an authoritative position when seeking information from a secret-keeper, the biggest disadvantage in those situations is that your position differentiates you (or sets you apart) from the secret-keeper. This sets up an immediate communications barrier that needs to be overcome in order to have the information shared. A communications barrier of this nature can cause an intellectual tug-of-war between *knowledge* (that they have) and *power* (that you have).

To better understand this concept, let's consider an example where an insurance company investigator needs to question a businessman (the secret-keeper) about a suspicious fire at his business. In this situation the insurance company investigator has a clear power advantage over the secret-keeper because if the investigator believes the businessman was involved in setting the fire, the claim may be refused or at least stalled. Regardless of whether the businessman is guilty or innocent, there is an intrinsic authoritative advantage weighted in favor of the investigator in this relationship; more so if the businessman is actually guilty.

For the sake of the example, let's consider the secret-keeper (businessman) is innocent. He has lost everything in the fire, been questioned by the police, by fire investigators and possibly the media. The businessman has had his entire life upturned and every aspect invaded by the authorities and now the insurance investigator is asking more questions. The person feels their private life as well as their business life has been trespassed on and he has suffered a distinct lack of privacy.

Despite the fact the person is innocent, he may not want to share any more information, particularly with yet another authoritative figure. The investigator just wants an accurate and truthful account of the circumstances. In this situation, even where the secret-keeper is innocent, if the investigator doesn't break down the communications barrier caused by the inherent authority difference, it's unlikely all will be revealed; it most definitely won't be revealed if the person were guilty of setting the fire.

Some people may consider the best way forward is for the insurance investigator to use their authority to *force* the secret-keeper to reveal the information; in this example, the threat of refusing or stalling an insurance payout may be held over the businessman's head. In some cases a stern approach can be a valid technique, in measured amounts in some circumstances. However, I don't support this approach as it rarely produces the most accurate and full account of circumstances. It usually results in half-truths and minimal information is provided by the secret-keeper to mitigate the threat. Once the threat is reduced the information stops flowing. We want voluntary and free flowing information to be forthcoming and threats rarely produce this.

Similarly teachers and parents can't yell at a troubled child and expect a deep and troubling secret to be revealed, fully and honestly. It may upset the child and some information may forcibly be revealed, but not fully and usually not accurately.

One of the main reasons why evidence obtained by the police under a threat is inadmissible in court is that pressuring and coercing information from people rarely works and, when it does, the information is inherently inaccurate and unreliable. The ineffectiveness of demanding and coercing information was highlighted in a study that sought the views and experiences of murderers and sexual offenders when interviewed by the police.[52]

The research compared two investigation styles used by the police; one dominating and forceful, and the other where the police approached the interview in a more humane and understanding way—communicating empathy and a genuine interest in the suspect and their predicament. The research was conclusive. More admissions were elicited as a result of the latter technique and less through forceful and coercive means, which only served to increase the number of lies and denials.

It was clear that even criminal offenders responded favorably and revealed their secrets when dealt with in a compassionate and understanding way. The results of this study have been replicated in several other similar studies and the majority of data indicates the ideal interviewer/elicitor is a person who can convey a range of emotions including empathy and sincerity during the information gathering process.[53] The consistent message here is that through positive verbal rapport and a demonstration of emotional empathy, even the most abhorrent offenders will reveal their secrets and willingly communicate the truth—even if it means going to gaol!

If murderers and sex offenders are prepared to confess incriminating evidence and in doing so ensure their conviction, then surely we can have others who don't face a gaol sentence tell us their hidden information? Yes we can; we just need to create the correct environment and a relationship that is conducive for information sharing and a major part of this is demonstrating empathy. Empathy is the identification with and understanding of another's situation, feelings and motives.[54] It's not sympathy; it's understanding the feelings of the other person.

In fact, research has shown that in police interviews, rapport building through empathy and sincerity increased cooperation in interviews and also the accuracy of recalled facts by 35–45%.[55] Regardless of the circumstances, when you are seeking hidden information from a position of authority or power, you will be more successful if you reduce the communications barriers and demonstrate empathy and sincerity.

Continuing with our example, if the insurance investigator (Dianne Johnson) introduced herself to the businessman like this, 'Hi, I'm Investigator Johnson. I need to ask you a few questions about the fire,' there are three immediate barriers created by that very first sentence.

- An authoritative *barrier,* by using the title 'investigator'
- A *personal barrier*, by using the surname 'Johnson'
- An *emotional barrier*, by a lack of empathy

This introduction drips with formality and authority and lacks emotional empathy which extinguishes any real potential for rapport with the secret-keeper; a vital ingredient in all elicitation processes. A simple change in that first sentence can set the wheels of rapport turning and may lead to the businessman providing not only just the required information, but much more.

A simple introduction of 'Hi, my name's Dianne. I work for Mackay Insurance. I'm sorry for your loss. Would you be willing to help me with some information?' would initiate a cooperative conversation and open the doors to hidden information far more effectively than an authoritative, officious and emotionally cold approach.

Even if the investigator suspects the businessman is guilty, it's important to erase the authority barrier verbally and show an emotional link through empathy. This is quickly done by dispensing the use of the 'investigator' title and using a first name only. The investigator's authority is inherent in the relationship and there is no advantage in reinforcing this verbally. If the businessman is guilty his guard may be lowered through a more empathetic approach as he won't feel like he is a suspect. If he is innocent there is an immediate emotional link with the insurance investigator, who has clearly demonstrated an understanding of the secret-keeper's predicament.

While this scenario used an insurance investigator, it could easily be a parent, doctor, teacher, counsellor, university lecturer or lawyer; in fact any situation where the secret-keeper perceives there is a difference in authority.

In direct elicitation situations, by relying upon professional expertise or positional authority, it's sometimes very easy to become adversarial with the person. This can very quickly result in a question and answer interview which won't produce the required full and accurate information. In these situations, first assess how you can dissolve any existing authoritative barrier and look for a way to demonstrate that you understand how the person feels; this will encourage a much more positive flow of hidden information.

Rapport is created through similarities; always minimise your differences and emphasise (even exaggerate) your similarities. Building a close rapport with a secret-keeper is the single most important element influencing whether a person will share hidden information.

Open-ended Questions

In direct elicitation situations, questions to be avoided are ones that result in a 'yes' or 'no' answer. When people are asked too many questions that simply require a 'yes' or 'no' response, the interaction quickly feels invasive or like an interrogation. Understandably, this can reduce their motivation for cooperation.

Questions that result in a 'yes' or 'no' answer are called 'closed questions' and while they do provide us some information, we want to elicit a lot more.

We want to use open-ended questions that evoke a response of some length from the secret-keeper—the longer the better. Research has shown that open-ended questions elicit longer and more detailed responses in police interviews.[56] These types of questions are gateways to conversations and evoke a response filled with information and importantly avoid the 'yes' or 'no' answer a closed question usually results in. Open-ended questions coax people to speak; it allows them an opportunity to tell you their story. These types of questions usually commence with single words or phrases such as:

- Who—Who were you with?
- What—What happened then?
- Why—Why did that happen?
- Where—Where did that information come from?
- When—When did the program commence?
- How—How did you meet?
- Can you tell me ...?
- Would you be able to explain ...?

As you can see, it's difficult to answer any of these questions with a blunt 'yes' or 'no' and places a conversational onus on the secret-keeper to give longer answers.

Closed versus Open-ended Questions

Closed	Open-ended
Parent: 'Did you go to the mall after school today?'	Parent: 'Can you tell me what you did after school today?'
Teenager: 'Yes'	Teenager: 'I went to the mall.'
Parent: 'Did you meet anyone there?'	Parent: 'What did you do there?'
Teenager: 'Yes'	Teenager: 'I met Mike and Dominique.'
Parent: 'Was it one of your friends?'	
Teenager: 'Yes'	Parent: 'What did you do then?'

Job interviewer: 'Are you a hard worker?' Applicant: 'Yes' Job Interviewer: 'Do you use initiative?' Applicant: 'Yes.' Job Interviewer: 'If you are hired, will you perform well?' Applicant: 'Yes.'	Job interviewer: 'Can you describe your work ethic?' Applicant: 'I'm a conscientious person who is punctual and dedicated to my role.' Job interviewer: 'If you are hired, how will you be able to help the company?'
Welfare counsellor: 'Have you done much since we last met?' Patient: 'No.' Or, Welfare counsellor: 'Did that make you feel angry?' Patient: 'Yes'	Welfare counsellor: 'Tell me what has happened since we last met.' Patient: 'Well ...' Or, Welfare counsellor: 'Can you explain how you felt when you saw that?' Patient: 'Well ...'

Before you ask a question in a direct elicitation situation, run it through your mind and assess if the answer can be 'yes' or 'no'. If it can be, simply rephrase it as an open-ended question.

Using Silence

On one occasion, a seasoned covert operative played me a recording of his very first undercover meeting. The meeting, during which he was to elicit particular information from a high-value target, took a long time to arrange, was resource intensive and was critical to the success of their overseas operation. The 20-minute recording of the meeting was full of clearly recorded conversation. The only problem was, the newly trained and very nervous covert operative babbled away constantly at the suspect throughout the entire meeting. The suspect barely said anything—he didn't have a chance! The conversation was full of the operative's valiant attempts at eliciting hidden information and they were technically well executed; if only he had stopped talking, the secret information would have flowed freely.[57]

This is not confined to cloak and dagger environments. Similar to the covert operative's unsuccessful elicitation attempt, a doctor or specialist who talks through most of the consultation and doesn't pause to listen to the patient is most likely to get the diagnosis wrong. This is not because of a lack medical expertise, but through conversational ineptitude. In addition to permitting an increase in the amount of patient information to assist with the diagnostic process, deliberate pauses by the doctor or specialist also allows an adequate time for the patient (secret-keeper) to mentally process a question and to provide a more cohesive response.

The more you talk when trying to elicit information, the less opportunity there is for the secret-keeper to share the hidden information. During any conversation, no one likes to be interrupted or, worse still, to have their sentences completed for them. After asking an open-ended question or setting your conversational 'hook' (discussed later in *Part Three*), it's best to pause, allow the secret-keeper to talk and take the position of being a good listener.

Most people will consider you are a great conversationalist if you simply ask questions and then listen to them do all the talking! People will naturally 'like' you if you give them a chance to be heard and actively listen and comment on what they have to say. People share more information with people they like.

So we've seen that silence can be a valuable tool to allow the secret-keeper to share information in a direct elicitation situation. Additionally, silence may also be used also to *cause* the secret-keeper to reveal information. When there is a silent pause in a conversation, people feel compelled to fill it with words (or even sounds!). You may have been to a presentation or event where a public speaker uses *umms* and *ahs* at the end of each sentence before commencing another. The primary reason for this is to avoid the deafening and uncomfortable silence. Silence may provoke a person in the audience to interrupt or make comment while the presenter is thinking of what to say next, so the person fills the space with *umm* and *ah* sounds. This allows the presenter to maintain conversational control as silence can be perceived as a conversational pass to another person, whose turn it is then to speak.

We have all been in situations where there is an awkward silence or pause during a conversation. The fact is, we simply don't enjoy pregnant pauses in these situations. When there is such a pause, one of the two people in the conversation will speak purely to relieve the uncomfortable silence; that person was forced into responding.

Using this phenomenon we can maintain our silence to provoke the secret-keeper to speak. Pauses are an important part of dialogue and 'pausing for effect' can be a useful tool in elicitation. Not just for emphasis, but importantly as a tool to encourage the secret-keeper to talk. Research has shown that the length of tolerable pauses in conversations varies between languages, cultures and the individuals engaged in the conversation. Broadly speaking, though, most of us can only tolerate pauses of two or three seconds before one of us simply has to speak.

A lengthy pause puts pressure on both people in the conversation. When a speaker finishes a sentence and then pauses and looks to the listener, the listener is under pressure to respond. If the speaker completes a statement and then the listener says nothing, the speaker will start to wonder if they have offended the listener or said something incorrect and will often clarify what they have said or add additional information. It is the latter example that is of real use when eliciting information.

When the secret-keeper tells you something, deliberately insert a pause. This provides little feedback to the secret-keeper and will create some psychological pressure to speak again. Keep in mind, though, that this technique should only be used sparingly as it can make the secret-keeper feel uncomfortable talking with you and may counter your rapport building efforts.

Indirect Elicitation

Indirect elicitation is, by its very nature, a more surreptitious activity than direct elicitation. With direct elicitation, secret-keepers are aware that you are attempting to obtain information and know they are being questioned, interviewed or asked about a particular issue. In contrast, one of the primary goals of indirect elicitation is to obtain information from people without them being aware. Unless a person has been specifically trained in counter-elicitation, or is extremely private and introverted, indirect elicitation is an effective tool on most people. By investing time and using a variety of techniques over a series of well-engineered conversations, it's possible to access most people's hidden information.

Some people may feel this all sounds sneaky and a bit untoward. Well, a book that's called *Unlocking Secrets* is bound to be a bit that way! In many elicitation processes there is a necessary element of deceit. However, it rarely goes beyond making simple conversational statements such as telling the secret-keeper that you like something or agreeing with their opinion when in fact you don't. These 'little white lies' occur as part of normal conversations every day, as people seek to cooperate and not offend others, e.g. 'Yes, I do like your new hair style' or 'Yes, you look like you've lost weight.'[58]

People are motivated to say these types of things so they don't unnecessarily offend a person. The only difference between this everyday deception and deception in elicitation is the motivation to create a relationship or a conversation for the purpose of learning hidden information.

Years ago when body language became the new frontier of interpersonal communications, some people considered the deliberate use of techniques such as 'mirroring' a person's body position, or deliberately using open body language techniques etc., to increase communication or feign interest in a conversation was also untoward.

Indirect elicitation is not a sinister practice, and it can form an important and proper part of parenting, teaching or business acumen as well as a person's social life. For example, parents often demand information on the spot from their child if they suspect the child of wrong-doing. Even if the parent uses the direct elicitation techniques discussed earlier, these attempts may fail. When a parent suspects a child is 'up to no good,' they rarely adopt a tailored strategy over a couple of conversations that will induce the child to tell-all. Conducted correctly, indirect elicitation can do this.

In a social context, indirect elicitation techniques may also be used as a dating tool to create a personal bond with another person very quickly. In business, indirect elicitation can identify when a competing company is making major decisions, its marketing strategies, secretly planned HR changes, or positive opportunities such as company expansion and impending promotional opportunities. Indirect elicitation can provide both protection and a vital personal or professional edge to the user.

Some professionals who teach elicitation to covert operatives would have you believe that it can only be conducted by experts and is far too complex for everyday people. I agree that indirect elicitation can be a very complex process, which is why I've designed the easy-to-follow READ Model of Elicitation. However, I disagree that everyday people can't be effective at unlocking secrets. All that is required is:

- Average intelligence
- Average interpersonal skills—a person with excellent interpersonal skills, or who likes talking to, or meeting new people will do extremely well
- Average self-confidence
- People observation skills—people who are perceptive of others or like watching other people (not stalkers!) will likely excel
- Life experience (age is an advantage; it's difficult for children to learn and apply these skills)
- A willingness to learn some basic knowledge and techniques (shown in this book)
- A preparedness to talk to people and to practise these skills

If you don't tick all these boxes, don't worry. I've seen some quite introverted people excel at elicitation simply with a bit of technical knowledge and some practice.

Indirect Elicitation Examples

- Meeting a competitor (secret-keeper) at a trade show or conference and having the person tell you some inside information to advantage your business.
- Police officer, workplace investigator, lawyer or private investigator eliciting additional information from a suspect, witness, or informant.
- Doctor, nurse, paramedic or welfare councillor using these skills to have a patient or client recall information that is suppressed or difficult for the person to manage.

- A negotiator may elicit vital information from the other side during apparent casual conversations
- In sales, these skills can be well utilized by both the retailer and the customer. The retailer may learn a great deal about the customer and then tailor the sales pitch accordingly to increase the chance of a sale. Similarly, the customer may use these skills to elicit information about the 'real' lowest price the item can be purchased for.
- A person considering purchasing a house may use indirect elicitation when speaking with other residents in the area to find out what it's really like living in that district.
- A parent may use these skills on another person when assessing that person's suitability to provide day care or private tuition for their child.

These are just some examples of where indirect elicitation may be used to advantage. However, the spectrum of where these skills may be utilized is only limited by the imagination.

In summary, indirect elicitation may be applied in any situation where you want to learn information from other people without them knowing.

Indirect Elicitation Techniques

In this section, we'll look at the most successful indirect elicitation technique aimed at subtly encouraging a secret-keeper to divulge their hidden information. It's called, 'being that person' and we'll learn how to do this using 'likeability,' 'emotional linking' and 'psychological mirroring'.

'Being That Person' using Likeability, Emotional Linking and Psychological Mirroring

As we have seen, some of the core skills used by spies and covert operatives are directly transferable to a variety of situations which can advantage and protect everyday people. Unlike spies, we can't (or shouldn't!) inject truth drugs such as sodium pentothal and sodium amytal to 'free the tongues' of people—but we can use conversational techniques and 'elicitation lines' that encourage a person to *willingly* and *voluntarily* share *accurate* information with us.

Fortunately, there are some aspects of human nature and secret-keeping that can assist us with this. For example, when a person has a secret there is an inherent and natural urge to want to share that information. Information sharing is our human default setting. In fact, it's rare that people will not tell at least one other person their hidden information; often they tell more than one person. This has been evidenced in recent research that verified very few people keep secrets just to themselves.[59] It is extremely rare that a person will not share. One study identified that in 87–96% of cases, people shared their emotional experiences rather than keeping them a secret.[60]

The urge to share is a natural desire to seek another perspective and gain some psychological relief by 'offloading' the information. This makes it difficult for people to keep secret information solely to themselves. So, in the correct circumstances, a secret will be revealed to at least one other person.

If we want to access that information, we need to create an environment and a relationship that encourages such a disclosure to us—we want to 'be that person' in the mind of the secret-keeper.

Coaxing not forcing

It's not possible to 'be that person' by being physically or verbally forceful (no thumb screws!). It's simply not possible to walk up to a business competitor and ask their company's tender price for a project, or demand to see their client list, nor can a person in the workplace successfully demand a senior manager to tell them the secret management plan for workplace redundancies. These attempts would simply fail.

Similarly, doctors, psychologists and counsellors would have very little success in demanding the most intimate details from clients. This type of information needs to be *coaxed* from people, even in these professional environments where trust is usually presumed and confidentiality is assured. If you were to visit one of these professionals and felt that they were asking more intimate questions than necessary and, importantly, you didn't 'like' the person, would you share your most confidential information with the specialist, or would you be more guarded? In that situation, many people would feel uncomfortable and not share even though it occurred in an environment where the professional is legally bound to keep information confidential. Why? Because the specialist is not 'being that person,' so you would be reticent to fully divulge your secret information.

If we want to 'be the person' the secret-keeper confides in, we need to know who secret-keepers confide in. We can then become 'that person' in the secret-keeper's mind. A unique study which examined the aspects of keeping and disclosing secrets of 70 people, provides us some excellent guidance on this very point.[61]

Of the 70 people who filled out the confidential questionnaires 41 stated they had a secret.[62] Of those 41, only 4 stated they had not told anyone their hidden information. So, in line with our earlier discussion, about 90% did disclose the information to at least one other person. The results of the study showed that most often, secrets were told to those who the secret-keeper felt *emotionally* close to. This was usually to 'friends or confidantes'—less so to people in the categories of family, partners and colleagues. Surprisingly, friends were about *three times* more likely to be confided in than family members or partners.[63]

To Whom Secrets are Told[64]

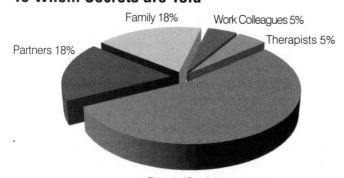

Family 18% Work Colleagues 5%

Therapists 5%

Partners 18%

Friends/Confidantes 54%

The fact that friends are confided in most often is good news for us, as it'll be almost impossible for you to suddenly become related to the secret-keeper and I don't recommend marrying a person just to access their secret—though it wouldn't be the first time this has happened in pursuit of international intelligence! However, if you become the secret-keeper's elicitation friend or confidante it is most likely the person will then share their hidden information.

To *become* 'that person' who is the friend or preferred confidante of the secret-keeper, you need to:

1. Be *liked by* the secret-keeper.
2. Have an *emotional link with* the secret-keeper.

Likeability

People share their most intimate and private information with people they 'like'. The more a secret-keeper likes you, the closer you'll become to 'being that person'. Regardless of how good your elicitation line is, if the secret-keeper doesn't like you, their information will remain locked away from you. Even after meeting very briefly, people get a sense of how they feel about another person very quickly. For this reason, we need to ensure that the first and also the last impression the secret-keeper has of you is a positive one of concurrence, i.e. you both agree on and share something and depart feeling positive about the interaction. This initial action sets the communication platform for that relationship at that particular point in time and will encourage more open and truthful communication to occur subsequently.

Most people have a natural sense of how to be likeable and friendly and most can turn on those charming interpersonal skills when they are required. We learn this from a very young age. Children are very adept at this and can change from demon to demure, from cranky to cute and from naughty to nice in a heartbeat, particularly when they want something! These skills develop as we grow and by the time we reach adulthood most of us are able to be likeable to another person when required, even if it's just for a short time. Even parking inspectors and debt collectors can be charming if they like ... maybe.

Using your natural ability to be 'likeable' is a good start for your interaction with the secret-keeper. However, in addition to being liked by the secret-keeper, the fastest way to encourage a person to share information also includes creating an emotional link.

Emotional linking

An emotional link may be formed between two people by a mutual point of interest, a commonality or a similar sense of humor and these are created quickly in situations where both people are in the same situation—and they feel emotionally similar. For example, the secret-keeper and the secret-target are waiting for a long time in a queue, when the secret-target shares how frustrating this is and then cracks a joke about the situation. If the secret-keeper laughs there is an established emotional link. Even if the joke falls flat, psychologically the secret-keeper will still acknowledge (internally) that they share the same emotion (frustration).

People relate better and communicate more effectively with those they consider are similar to themselves. In this case, indicating the same emotion as the secret-keeper demonstrates similarity and creates a subtle mental alliance. In the secret-keeper's mind, the secret-target thinks similarly and understands the situation the same way as the secret-keeper. This creates an emotional link, not a strong one, but there is a shared emotion between the two and that is a great starting point. When this is done deliberately, it's called psychological mirroring.

Psychological mirroring

Psychological mirroring works on the well-proven premise that 'people like people who are like them'. Psychological research demonstrates that people share information more readily with people who have similar characteristics, such as age, values, beliefs and culture.[65] This doesn't mean we can't communicate or don't enjoy communicating with people who are different from us, but on most occasions we feel more comfortable divulging information to people who have something in common with us. This human trait is not limited to major characteristics. For example, two people of different cultures may have increased relatedness when one of them highlights that they are both members of the same church, sporting club, or on the same side of politics. However, if one of them was to point out all the differences between them rather than the similarities, close communication becomes difficult and would attenuate the free flow of information!

One study even demonstrated that using similar names on envelopes produced a more positive response from people.[66] This study posted questionnaires (asking for a response) to people using a sender's name similar to the recipient. For example, a questionnaire sent to Joan Read had a (false) sender's name of John Ready. The study showed that when the recipient's name was mirrored by the sender details, the return rate increased to 56% from 30% (when the recipient's name was not mirrored). A significant aspect is that this increase occurred without any interpersonal communication, simply a similar name written on paper. When we use the technique of psychological mirroring in person it's even more influential!

In a body language context, there is a substantial amount of evidence that 'physically mirroring' another person's body position enhances interpersonal communication. Recent research has demonstrated that *behavior mirroring* increased trust during negotiations and this led to the 'mirrored' person disclosing details more readily to the person who was mirroring, and another study showed that mirroring increased sales from 12.5% to 67%![67]

Psychological mirroring takes the body language mirroring concept further and seeks to tap into the psychological bias to favor those that are similar to us. By demonstrating the same emotion as the secret-keeper in the same situation we can establish an emotional link. Unlike body language it's not just the physical mirroring that is critical; it's psychological 'mirroring' of the secret-keeper.

Psychological mirroring is deliberately demonstrating and sharing the same emotion as the secret-keeper at the same time. This is very effective at creating rapid emotional rapport between two total strangers and frees the flow of information very quickly.

With all elicitation situations it's important to demonstrate clearly through speech and actions that we understand and, importantly, share the secret-keeper's emotions about the given situation. Regardless of the circumstances, whether it's happy, sad, exciting or funny, we need to tune-in to the secret-keeper's emotions at the time we engage with them and demonstrate our understanding of whatever emotion they are experiencing at that time.

One effective way to do this is by using similar or the same words and phrases as the secret-keeper. For example, if the secret-keeper says, 'It's so hot today!,' your response should be, 'Yes, you're right it is really hot.' Not: 'Yes, it's very humid today.' By using a different term (humidity) the secret-keeper may conclude that you are either showing a different perception of the same situation, or deliberately using a more technical word, as some kind of one-upmanship—both are counter to bringing the secret-keeper closer to us.

Repeating words or phrases used by the secret-keeper during the conversation reinforces the similarities between you.

If you reflect upon your past experiences, there may have been an occasion when you were in a group of strangers and for some reason you all shared the same emotional experience. Perhaps, you may have been waiting for hours in an airport departure lounge, or been on a bus or aircraft that broke down or was diverted. Perhaps you were seated next to another person in a restaurant when the two of you each had to wait a very long time for your meals to arrive. If a stranger in the same situation as you was nice to you, i.e. while in the departure lounge they lent you a magazine or mobile phone to contact relatives about your later arrival time, and the stranger was empathetic (showing they shared the same feelings about the situation), and days later you saw each other again would you still be strangers? I suspect if you met on a second occasion, there would be, a nod, a slight smile or at least a minor acknowledgement as there is now a kinship (albeit weak) between you. You like the person because of the kind gesture and you have an emotional link as you both felt the same emotion about the same situation at the same time.

In situations like this people feel psychologically similar and on the same side against a common adversity. Even smokers who, through their working day stand outside the workplace in rejected groups, form an emotional bond and share information more readily as a result. Strangely enough, some lifelong friendships have been born out of these types of situations! They provide a similar experience to team building exercises which are aimed at creating bonds through shared experiences.

In a different context, camaraderie is very quickly formed with police, emergency services workers and military personnel when dealing with tragic and personally testing experiences, because they traverse through the same emotions together and form a close emotional bond. Psychological mirroring replicates this.

Regardless of whether it's a positive or a negative experience, it's critical for us to overtly and clearly demonstrate our 'shared' emotional experience, because (in the secret-keeper's mind), it brings the secret-keeper emotionally closer to us. This enhances the relationship rapport and paves the way for closer, more intimate communications.

Psychological mirroring: Two mirrors in a lift

On one occasion I was in an elevator with a number of people, including an elderly lady and a suited businessman, when the lift inexplicably stopped. No one likes being stuck in a lift and this situation affects different people differently. We waited in silence for a few minutes, hoping the lift would spring to life again. When it didn't, one of the other people used the elevator phone to contact security, who promised a technician would have the elevator mobile again shortly.

After a few minutes, on my left, the elderly lady began showing signs of fear and anxiety and on my right the businessman was already making huffing sounds and regularly checking his watch; clearly he needed to be somewhere by a particular time. Apart from a minor time inconvenience, being stuck in the lift had no impact on me. Regardless, I turned to the elderly lady and told her that I get a bit tense in situations like this as it's a bit unsettling (psychological mirror one). She told me that she also felt that way. I told her that I think a lot of people feel that way (normalising statement), but really there was little to be worried about and shortly we'd all be on our way (reassurance). The elderly lady gave me a genuine smile.[68]

Moments later, I turned to the businessman and adjusted my psychological mirror and told him that I hated things like this happening and that it was a real inconvenience as I was on my way to a specialist's appointment and now I may be late. He remained stony faced, but agreed and said he was on his way to the airport. I complained to him that I don't know why in the 21st century we can't make shopping trolleys that go straight or lifts that don't break down. After a few more exchanges, I could see his mood lifting. So I adjusted my mirror to reflect this in my conversation with him by making less cynical and more light-hearted comments. His mood improved further.

A short time later, the lift technician's voice came through the speaker in the wall next to the businessman and told us all that we would be moving in a few minutes. I then asked the businessman if he could order me a cheeseburger meal (as if it were a McDonald's drive through speaker) and this really amused him. Then, without prompting, he started telling me how important it was for him to make his flight as he had a meeting with a prospective investor. Through psychological mirroring, in his mind we were on the same emotional journey starting with frustration and ending with humor. Now he wasn't a secret-keeper as far as I was concerned, as I had no interest in what his business plans were—but if I was, this would have been a great way to start eliciting information from him.

A few moments later the elevator started to move and everyone's mood lifted. As we all exited, despite the fact that he was running late the businessman took the time to say goodbye. Then he extended his hand and we shook hands. Fifteen minutes earlier we got into a lift and he didn't acknowledge me or anyone else. Now he wanted to shake hands with a stranger when he was late to the airport. Why? Because we were no longer strangers;we had an emotional link created by psychological mirroring.

If we had met again shortly after this incident, our conversation would have started more as friends than strangers, though this would decay with the passing of time. To make sure we started a new interaction as warmly as the other one concluded I would use an elicitation hook and elicitation syncher (explained in *Part Three*). For example, a hook of 'Have you been caught in any lifts lately?' would immediately get his attention. Then I'd select an elicitation syncher such as 'So have you got my cheeseburger yet?' This would tie our new conversation directly to the humorous incident and the positive emotional link that formed in the elevator.

As I left the building, I said goodbye to the elderly lady, who then thanked me for helping her. She was clearly never a secret-keeper from my perspective and I used psychological mirroring to comfort her. Nevertheless, an emotional link had been formed between us.

In summary, people share hidden information with at least one other person. With indirect elicitation, if you can be 'likeable' and successfully psychologically mirror a secret-keeper by demonstrating your shared emotional experience, an emotional link will be formed and you will be well on the way to 'being that person'.

PART TWO KEY POINTS

To serve as a memory aid, below I have listed the key points from *Part Two* for easy reference.

- Elicitation is a conversation that is deliberately conducted with a specific learning agenda. It is a conversation with the subtle purpose of gaining information.

- Through skilful elicitation, a great deal may be learned from the person of interest, who if questioned directly would refuse to provide that information.

- Elicitation is part of our everyday lives, and those most effective at it gain the most advantage and best protection as a result of those skills.

- Elicitation is *not* about intimidation or coercing information from a person, nor is it about causing the person to fabricate information; it's about uncovering the truth which is wrapped up in a secret form.

- The most critical element in all elicitation efforts is establishing a close rapport with the secret-keeper.

- If we elicit the information correctly, it will be an enjoyable conversation for both the secret-keeper and the secret-target (that's you).

Direct elicitation

- Direct elicitation is a process where the secret-keeper is aware that you are attempting to gain access to their hidden information. This can occur in structured settings, such as an interview-like situation, or in other less formal environments. However, it remains an inquisitive process where the person knows you are attempting to learn their hidden information.

- Direct elicitation may assist in many situations such as:

- Parents or teachers asking children about an incident the child witnessed but perhaps don't want to implicate their friend, or possibly reveal their own misbehavior (to avoid self-incrimination).

- Welfare situations; such as parents, teachers or counsellors or medical professionals asking about hidden traumatic information, such as being a victim of crime, road accidents, bullying, grief counselling, etc.

- Medical practitioners asking patients questions about information the patient may not want to volunteer freely, such as illegal drug use, smoking, hidden eating disorders, excessive drinking, etc.

- Police officers, investigators and security personnel questioning a suspect, informant or a witness.

- Direct elicitation strategies include:

  - Avoiding a stalemate: Asking questions with wriggle room so the person doesn't back himself into a corner.

  - Dissolving authority barriers and demonstrating emotional empathy: Quickly build a rapport with the person and have them open up to you.

  - Asking open-ended questions: So the person cannot shut the conversation down with a simple yes or no answer.

  - Using silence: Causing the person to speak.

- If you are in a direct elicitation process, avoid relying on any positional authority you have to force the truth from the secret-keeper. Studies have shown that a person who can demonstrate empathy and sincerity will access hidden information far more effectively.

Indirect elicitation

- Indirect elicitation is, by its very nature, a more surreptitious activity than direct elicitation. The primary goal of indirect elicitation is to learn hidden information from a person, without that person being aware.

- Indirect elicitation can form an important and proper part of a parenting, teaching, business planning and a person's social life.

- Indirect elicitation may assist with:

  - Meeting a competitor (secret-keeper) at a trade show or conference and having the person tell you some inside information to advantage your business.

  - Police officer, workplace investigator, lawyer or private investigator eliciting additional information from a witness, or informant.

  - Doctor, nurse, paramedic or welfare councillor using these skills to have a patient or client recall information that is suppressed or difficult for the person to manage.

  - A negotiator may elicit vital information from the other side during apparent casual conversations

- The most successful indirect elicitation strategy is 'being that person' and it's achieved using:

  - Likeability: people share their most intimate and private information with people they 'like'. The more a secret-keeper likes you, the closer you'll become to 'being that person.'

- Emotional linking: An emotional link is formed by a mutual point of interest, a commonality or a similar sense of humor and these are created quickly in situations where both people are in the same situation—and they feel emotionally similar.

- Psychological mirroring: Sharing an emotional journey creates emotional bonds. Psychological mirroring recreates this and can cause a bond to form very quickly between two complete strangers.

- The greatest threat to successfully unlocking a secret is appearing insincere. The greatest asset is being liked and sharing an emotional link or closeness.

- Emotional links created by psychological mirroring decay with time. If you use this technique, it's important that you re-engage the secret-keeper shortly after you have created the link to cement a more permanent information-sharing relationship.

Part Three:

Getting Engaged—Hook, Line and Syncher

In *Part Four*, we'll find out how to use the READ Model of Elicitation. Before we do that, we need to learn how to effectively 'engage' a secret-keeper as this is the most important stage of the model.

We've already learned that people with hidden information will share that information with at least one other person; usually a friend or confidante and always a person the secret-keeper feels close to and likes. Close engagement is the fastest and most effective way to achieve this status in the mind of the secret-keeper.

There are three steps to follow to rapidly engage a person with hidden information. These are:

- **Elicitation hook**: A conversational technique to immediately 'hook' the secret-keeper into a conversation.

- **Elicitation line**: A technique or strategy used to influence a secret-keeper to open up (beyond the hook) and talk with you.

- **Elicitation syncher**: To SYNCHronise the positive feelings and close rapport from one conversation to a later conversation.

In the following sections, we'll take a closer look at each of these engagement stages and you'll see how easy and effective these can be. As humans are psychologically complex there is no one-size-fits-all elicitation technique. All situations are different and all secret-keepers are individuals, so in this part I'd like to provide you with a variety of psychological tools to enhance your chance of success. This way you can tailor your engagement approach depending upon your relationship with the secret-keeper, the circumstances of the meeting and the type of information you are trying to access.

If you follow the hook, line and syncher method, you'll be amazed at how quickly you can become a person's close friend and confidante. This is not only a useful technique in an elicitation context; it can also result in very effective networking and even enhance personal relationships!

The Right Hook for the Right Fish

An 'elicitation hook' is a conversational technique used to immediately hook the secret-keeper into a conversation. It's to get you past 'Hi' and into a conversation.

The elicitation hook needs to make the secret-keeper reply. Where possible, an elicitation hook should consist of two parts:

1. A statement (you both agree upon); followed by

2. An adjoining question (to prompt the secret-keeper into talking with you).

To select a hook, use your human instinct, life skills and observations of the environment and of the secret-keeper to assess what is the most important issue on the mind of the secret-keeper at that particular time. That way you will be able to tailor your opening statement with something that you both agree on and then insert your question to evoke a response. This should make selecting a hook easy.

The most basic example of this process is a simple comment on the weather. For this most basic conversation starter, a statement such as, 'It's cold today' won't work as the hook doesn't have a question component. Without the question part of the hook the conversation may be stop at 'yes.' A hook needs to start the conversation flowing.

Here's the same simple idea reworded into an effective hook that seeks the secret-keeper's opinion: 'It's cold today. Do you think it was this cold last year?' However, a hook like this does not work on busy people (who are not interested in the weather at the particular time and are concentrating on other issues) or a person who is in a warm environment (as cold is not at the forefront of their thinking at that time). However, a hook such as this will work on a cold day at a bus stop, when people have time (waiting for the bus) and are affected by the weather as the cold conditions are foremost in their thoughts at that time.

The elicitation hook in action

Imagine you were walking along the street with a group of colleagues for a business lunch and you wanted hidden information from a senior manager (the secret-keeper) in the group. The senior manager is visiting from Sydney and had just done a HR efficiency review for the company CEO, who was soon to announce major changes for the company based on that very report. None of you have met the senior manager before.

As you are all walking along, the senior manager kicks her toe on a raised piece of pavement. What's your response? You may want to laugh but this wouldn't help your elicitation efforts! You quickly see this as an opportunity and assess what's in the forefront of her mind at that time. Using psychological mirroring and a hook, you show her your frustration and say, 'The local council should do something about the state of the footpaths in this place. I kicked my toe near here last week and wrecked a good pair of shoes. Are they this bad in Sydney?'

This would work well as a hook because pain, frustration, possibly embarrassment and the state of her shoes will be at the forefront of her mind. You and the secret-keeper agree on a common point, are clearly both on the same side and the hook causes her to reply with, 'No! They are much better in Sydney.' You agree with her by saying, 'Well, I've visited Sydney plenty of times and never had a problem. I'm going to write to the local council about what happened to us and see if I can get some action.' Using the term 'us' unites the two of you further and cements you as being on the same side.

While your next questions won't be, 'Can you tell me about the confidential findings of your report?' or, 'What's the CEO going to say in his speech?' or even 'Is my job safe?', you now have an edge that no one else in the group has; an emotional link with the senior manager. You can then build upon this by using elicitation lines and elicitation synchers (explained in the next section) during the lunch. This will provide you with some fantastic insight into the senior manager and rapidly accelerate the already initiated rapport between you. Over a few subsequent conversations, you should be able to access the type of information you require, and secret information in the future.

The process of being 'likeable' using psychological mirroring and an elicitation hook applies in every situation. For example, if you observe a happy looking and energetic secret-keeper tapping their foot in time to the music in a bar or café, a happy and energised hook (psychological mirror) you could use is: 'Hey, they play great music in this place, don't they? Is it usually so good here?'. This should evoke a conversational response. Similarly, if the secret-keeper has been standing in a queue or waiting for their order for some time, a frustrated and impatient (psychological mirror) hook of, 'They need to improve the service in this place! Have you been waiting long?' should do the trick.

An effective hook causes the secret-keeper to immediately agree with your opening statement (you are non-threatening, have something in common and are on the same side), then importantly your question seeks their opinion, which (in their mind) verifies they are considered important to you and unless they are straight out rude, they must engage in conversation with you.

When unlocking hidden information, all conversation (both emotionally positive and negative) coming from a secret-keeper is better than silence. However, it's important that by the time the conversation is over, that secret-keeper reflects favorably on both you and the conversation. This will make the next planned conversation between you that much easier because when the person sees you, it will recreate in their mind the feelings of your last engagement.

If you cast your hook and the secret-keeper is abrupt, gruff or dismissive, don't be discouraged; continue with your psychological mirroring. Once you feel you have established an emotional link, steer the conversation towards a more light-hearted subject area if possible, to round off your conversation that way.

We all like happy endings, but this is not always possible when a secret-keeper is difficult to communicate effectively with. All is far from lost though, because even if your encounter was frustrating, this doesn't necessarily mean that the secret-keeper will immediately associate you directly with that frustrating experience. If your elicitation hook and elicitation lines have been effective, the secret-keeper's recall will not focus primarily on the frustration, but that you both endured the situation together—that in itself is a positive.

In summary, your hook should consist of two parts. First, use your psychological mirror technique; an opening statement of commonality (something you both agree on that places you both on the same side) that is at the forefront of the secret-keeper's mind. Second, acknowledge the secret-keeper's worth by asking a question (seeking an opinion). This should initiate a positive start to your interaction with the person. Steer the conversation towards a positive conclusion if you can.

Having a good hook almost always helps you avoid being brushed off by the secret-keeper. This then allows you to progress and use your elicitation line.

Casting Your Elicitation Line

An elicitation line is a technique or strategy used to influence a secret-keeper to open up (beyond the hook) and talk with you. Elicitation lines exploit some natural human tendencies such as:

- People are generally polite and want to be helpful, even when they are asked questions by (friendly) strangers.

- Most want to appear well informed and will share information to demonstrate this.

- Sharing information, including secrets, is a natural human default position with secrets almost always being shared (87–96%) with at least one other person—usually a friend or confidante the secret-keeper feels emotionally close to.

- Everyone wants to feel appreciated or acknowledged in some way.

- If we are given something, including invitations, gifts and even information, most often we feel an obligation to return the favor.

- When a person is provided exclusive access to someone's secret, they feel flattered, more trusted and closer to that person.

When engaging with the secret-keeper, you may choose to use just one or a combination of lines throughout the conversation. You'll definitely notice when you are using the correct line, as the secret-keeper will 'light up' and really start to talk to you. This is the first phase of the READ Model of Elicitation—'research and assess' (discussed in more detail in *Part Four*). The purpose of this phase is to provide an insight into the secret-keeper to help you select an elicitation hook which causes the person to talk with you. The elicitation line follows very closely on from the hook. An elicitation line's primary purpose is to continue the conversation to:

- Strengthen the emotional link
- Rapidly build rapport
- Bring you closer to the secret-keeper
- Allow you to steer the conversation to the secret subject area
- Elicit the secret information, if possible

Elicitation lines discussed in this section make use of the following tactics:

- Flattery
- Sharing a secret secret to uncover a real secret
- Quid pro quo—reciprocity
- Disbelief
- False statement
- I'll never see you again
- Pick a common enemy
- Exclusively yours!
- Gee, you really are important, please tell me more!

Flattery

There is no secret that flattery is commonly used by individuals to gain favor or advantage with another person. Compliments are often handed out, with the obvious purpose of making the receiver feel good about the person offering the compliment. We all enjoy being flattered about something, but only when it's genuine. When flattery is delivered insincerely it always has a negative impact.

An obvious example of false flattery

Teenager: 'Hi Mum. You look nice today; have you lost weight?'

Mum: 'Oh thanks, I have lost a bit of weight and I did my hair differently today.'

Teenager: 'Can I borrow the car?'

Mum: 'No!'

By contrast, you may have been in a situation where someone gave you a *genuine* compliment about something you had done or the way you looked, for example; and it understandably made you feel good and more positive about yourself and also about that person. For this reason flattery can be a useful elicitation line. You may have also been in a situation where someone gave you a compliment and you instinctively knew it was false or said to you for a specific purpose. In this situation, that person loses credibility and trust. For this reason, flattery is also a dangerous elicitation line. It's important to keep in mind that 'false flattery fails' and is obvious to most people.

Because people do encounter flattery with a hidden agenda more often, people are more practised at identifying it. Therefore if you decide to use flattery, you need it to be a genuine compliment. In my opinion, unless a person is earnestly seeking a compliment, in which case they won't critically assess such a comment, flattery is difficult to use convincingly as an elicitation line. The trick to doing so is to genuinely compliment the secret-keeper on something that you truly believe. Alternatively, you must be very subtle about how you offer the compliment.

Remember that the purpose of an elicitation line is to strengthen the emotional link, to build rapport and to bring you closer to the secret-keeper. An obvious use of false flattery will destroy that very quickly. Additionally, we have seen that secret-keepers share information with those they feel close to. If a secret-keeper believes you are insincere, they won't feel close to you and simply won't share information; in fact, any further conversation with you will likely be cold or strained and remain at a superficial level.

While acknowledging there are inherent difficulties in using flattery, when offered effectively it works very well. Unlike the previous example we should never offer a compliment directly and then dive into a different subject area, particularly one where we are asking for secret information. Flattery needs to be delivered in small amounts and where possible it should focus on the secret subject area. When delivered convincingly in this way, it ties the person's good feeling about you to the secret subject area and raises their level of tolerance to talk about that subject.

You may find this hard to believe, but most senior managers, even CEOs and VPs, are ripe for the picking when it comes to flattery. Not upfront flattery such as 'Gee I like your suit!' or 'Your speech was really inspiring.' This is far too obvious and people who reach these types of positions are generally (not always!) quite clever and most have highly developed and perceptive interpersonal skills. However, this group is particularly vulnerable to flattery.

Because these people have likely represented their company at industry conferences, trade shows or shareholders meetings and given very high level company presentations and client pitches, they feel they are a vital part of the company and what it stands for. Most often these people are also well paid and understandably very proud of, and loyal to, their company. The best way to use flattery on these people is to compliment the company they work for as they will automatically adopt the compliment as their own. They do this because psychologically they link the company and their position to their own identity. So, if you compliment the company, they psychologically interpret this as their own personal compliment.

As people are usually aware of false flattery, it's always safer to deliver flattery via a third party or in parallel to what the secret-keeper does, likes or associates with. This could be complimenting the secret-keeper's company, industry skills, sporting code or even the breed of their dog. When flattery is delivered this way, the person is more accepting and less suspicious because the person associates closely with whatever you are complimenting; they take the compliment as their own, which gives them a positive feeling towards you. Remember people share information with people they like—and we naturally like those who like us.

Using Compliments

If you were fortunate enough to have created a revolutionary new internet search tool and wanted to learn some inside information from a senior manager at Google you wouldn't start by telling the person that Bing is a great search tool!

Instead, you'd try a flattery elicitation line something like this: 'I remember what internet searching was like before Google and it was clumsy and ineffective. Google changed all that. What you guys have done at Google has really changed the internet world forever. Your technology must be cutting edge.'

This should result in the person feeling more positive about you. Regardless of whether the person was actually working for Google when it commenced, the secret-keeper will take this line as a personal compliment. Additionally, it ties that compliment directly to the area you are seeking information about; technology.

Regardless of the industry or business type, flattery will most often work (in measured amounts) with secret-keepers in senior positions when the compliment is delivered surreptitiously via their company.

There are many ways to deliver a flattery elicitation line without it being obvious and direct. Consider this situation: you are at work and a senior manager/partner who is always very busy and has a phone to his ear most of the day, asks if you could meet in his office for a few minutes. As you enter the office he greets you with a smile and you realize you aren't about to be sacked! Then he says, 'I really want your opinion on something, but please wait a second while I turn off my phone so we won't be interrupted.' If this 'very important and busy person' was cutting off all outside communications and was clearly planning to give you his undivided attention so he could listen to your opinion, how would that make you feel? Most people in that situation would feel valued—this is indirect flattery.

Perhaps you are a supervisor, workplace assessor or manager of people. If you wanted to unlock someone's secret at work, simply and deliberately turning off your phone in front of the person when you meet is a subtle and effective flattery elicitation line. There are limitless ways you can use a flattery elicitation line (without giving an obvious and direct compliment) that the person will 'interpret' as a personal compliment. This way the secret-keeper feels more positive about you, yet your purposeful and deliberate flattery has been disguised.

Workplace flattery

To a hairdresser: 'It takes a lot of skill to be a good hairdresser. There's a lot more to it than holding scissors and a hairdryer.'

To a truck driver: 'People forget that without truck drivers the nation would come to a standstill.'

To a stay-at-home parent: 'I find it so incredible that there is so much emphasis on having a career when being at home to raise your children is so important.'

Another good way to use a subtle flattery elicitation line is to focus on people's work ethic. Most people believe they work hard (even authors think this—how bizarre!) and a large majority also feel the work they do is important. So on most occasions you will receive a positive response by tailoring your flattery elicitation line to how important a particular vocation is or how hard people in the secret-keeper's industry work.

Job flattery

To a newspaper reporter: 'I find it amazing that people just expect their newspaper to be full of the latest error-free news every day. Do you think they ever stop and think that someone actually had to research and write that information and also meet deadlines?'

To a paramedic: 'There's always so much written about how hard doctors work. People forget that ambulance officers and paramedics are the ones in the field who work at the sharp end.'

In summary, as people are quite adept at identifying false flattery, this elicitation line is best delivered indirectly and only used in measured amounts. When cast in a subtle way, the person will feel more positive about you and will be more inclined to share information with you.

Sharing a Secret Secret to Uncover a Real Secret

In *Part One* we discussed how two people in a secret relationship share secret information and exclude all others. We also found that this form of secrecy forms a social bond of considerable strength between the two secret-keepers. In various studies, it was established that sharing a secret can increase the attraction with, and closeness between, the two people who share a secret.[69] This is primarily because shared secrets require reciprocal trust between the two secret-keepers.

So when one person initiates and shares a secret with another, it communicates both trust and closeness to the receiver. This then has a natural influence on the receiver to reciprocate that trust and closeness. Studies also demonstrated that the nature and content of the secret was largely irrelevant; it was the process of being secretive that created a feeling of close relatedness.[70]

Putting all this together, if we are able to share our own secret with the secret-keeper (regardless of what it's about) and form a secret relationship, that person will in turn share secret information. This doesn't mean a 'personal' relationship such as dating or sleeping with the secret-keeper; that would be unethical. However, by sharing our own secret (regardless of what it is about) with the secret-keeper, that person will feel flattered, closer and more trusted. The secret-keeper will psychologically assess that the relationship has developed to a more emotionally close and trustworthy partnership. This can rapidly set the platform for a more sharing relationship.

Consider how you would feel if a friend said to you, 'I've never told anyone this before but ...' and the person told you some very significant information. Understandably you would feel privileged and also closer to the person because from your perspective, of all the people the friend knows, you were chosen above all others as the only one worthy to be allowed access to this most secret information.

You can open an otherwise locked psychological gate by sharing a personal secret of your own if you are attempting to unlock hidden information from a close friend, patient or client of a sensitive and intimate nature. This can also minimise the person's shame or negativity about sharing their information. Using direct or indirect elicitation to share a very private (true or untrue) secret to form a closer bond with the secret-keeper can greatly assist a person who has difficulty relaying their feelings and experiences.

Never share a secret with secret-keepers about another person, as it may cause them to reflect upon whether you can keep their information secret.

If you want to reinforce just how confidential you keep information without saying 'trust me' (as this never works!), try, 'Well, someone told me something confidential about that, but I can't talk about it because I said I wouldn't tell anyone.' This is far more effective as the secret-keeper will use statements like this as a benchmark when measuring your trustworthiness and assessing whether to trust sharing information with you.

Sharing secrets

If a welfare officer who previously suffered from bulimia is having difficulty assisting a client (secret-keeper) to open-up about their own eating disorder, the welfare officer may say, 'I don't ever tell my clients this, but when I was a teenager I suffered from bulimia.' Or 'Please keep this to yourself because I never tell anyone, but years ago I went through a terrible phase of bingeing on food then taking laxatives to try to make sure I didn't gain weight.' Statements like this may be used even when they are untrue. However, they remain just as effective as they shout out to the secret-keeper that there is a special and close sharing aspect to the relationship.

In this example, it doesn't really matter what the subject of the welfare officer's secret is as long as it's a private secret that's been exclusively divulged to the secret-keeper. It may be about the welfare officer's own difficulties dealing with bullying, a secret about their childhood, or even their financial situation. What's critical from the secret-keeper's perspective is the fact that the welfare officer has shared their own deepest secret. This encourages the secret-keeper to consider doing the same, because that is now the nature of that relationship. It becomes a secret relationship and this can form a bond of sharing information.

In elicitation it's preferable to share secret information of the same type that you are seeking—this is explained in the next section—however, it is not always necessary. As long as the secret-keeper believes you have shared a closely guarded secret, it forms the basis of a secret relationship and will bring you closer to sharing more intimate information. To suit this purpose you may choose to fabricate a secret or tell a genuine secret.

Examples of secret sharing

- An employee shares a 'secret' with a supervisor to add an additional aspect to the otherwise work-only relationship, so that the supervisor then shares secret information about management decisions. Conversely, sharing a secret with an employee may gain the supervisor information from the employee's work level perspective.

- With the view to accessing hidden information about a competitor's company, a company employee at a trade show shares a fabricated intimate secret with a friendly competitor to create an impression that the relationship is closer than it actually is.

- Under the guise of a customer in a bar, a private investigator (who is hired by a suspicious wife) confides in the husband the 'secret' that he (the private investigator) is having an affair. In return, the husband also confides.

- When dating, one person shares a very deep and emotional secret with the view to having the prospective partner open up and share more intimate information. When this occurs, a secret relationship is created and there is most often an increase in attraction and closeness.

Quid Pro Quo—Reciprocity

Quid pro quo means 'this for that,' or 'a favor given for a favor returned,' e.g. you scratch my back, I'll scratch yours. This may be a business-like agreement, e.g. 'If I do this for you (or your company) then I expect you to do this for me.' It can also be transactional such as when a person pays money and receives a product or service in return for their payment, or when a parent pays a child some pocket money when the child has finished cleaning their room (not before!).

While quid pro quo can apply in both the business and the transactional forms, it also manifests naturally in society. For example, when a couple invites another couple to their house for dinner, the invited couple feels a necessary obligation to return the favor. Similarly, if a person unexpectedly brought you a coffee while you were at work, you would likely feel an obligation to return that kind gesture. This very positive aspect of human nature usually results in a person repaying the kindness with a similar gesture.

Using the previous example, it would be unlikely that you would return the favor of the cup of coffee by buying a lottery ticket for the person, even if it cost the exact same amount of money. This is because it's not the *cost* of the favor you are returning, it's the favor itself. It's best returned in the same or similar form. Similarly, if your neighbor collected your mail for you when you were on holiday and you learned s/he was going on holiday, you would want to return that same favor or a similar one.

We usually prefer to return a favor in a similar form, but when we can't we'll repay the favor anyway. For example, during one research program, people were given an unsolicited can of cola by a person and sometime later that day were approached by that same person selling raffle tickets. Those who had been given the complimentary can of drink purchased twice as many raffle tickets as the people who were not given one—such is the strength of quid pro quo.[71]

Faced with a quid pro quo obligation, in the absence of a similar commodity to the can of cola, they bought raffle tickets to satisfy that obligation.

This attribute of human nature is important from an elicitation perspective as it also applies to information exchange. Consider a working relationship you have with a person that is based purely on getting the work done. You are friendly and get on well, but you only meet at work and only discuss work-related matters. One Monday morning the person starts to tell you about what they did on the weekend. It's likely that in that situation you would reciprocate and at least tell the person something about your weekend. In return for the person sharing information about their weekend you would feel obligated to do the same.

To assist in unlocking a secret, we can give a person some information—of the same or similar kind that we want from the secret-keeper. This isn't approached in a transactional way. For example, at a software trade show you would not state outright: 'Our company is planning to diversify into a new market of gaming, is yours?' Most secret-keepers would feel uncomfortable and defensive about this very stark approach, particularly if the person is very loyal to their company. We want to tell the secret-keeper some information so that they feel obligated to volunteer information to us about a similar subject.

Taking a lesson from the previous section on sharing a secret secret to unlock a real secret, a better approach would be: 'Please keep this just between you and me, but my company is planning to diversify into gaming, away from our core business.' Then you need to pause—forcing the secret-keeper to make a comment about this secret information. In that situation, depending on how well you have developed a rapport with the person, the secret-keeper will feel obligated to also share a secret of the same kind. They might say: 'Well, my bosses decided a similar thing a few months ago and we are now moving towards developing voice recognition platforms and this has diverted a lot of our resources away from our normal work.'

A combination of sharing a secret and quid pro quo causes a secret-keeper to feel increased closeness and the need to share a secret of the same or similar nature.

Scenarios of secret sharing and quid pro quo

At a large pharmaceutical conference, Stan and Simon coincidently meet at the free buffet lunch. Stan wants to access hidden information from Simon. They have met several times before at similar conferences. Despite working for competing firms, they are friendly with each other and decide to sit together at lunch. On Stan's suggestion they agree to meet after the conference at a bar for a social drink.

Stan has deliberately engineered the meeting at a bar, so he can meet Simon in a social and relaxed environment away from the conference area which would only serve to remind Simon that he is representing his company and part of that is the requirement to avoid disclosing confidential information.

At the bar that night, Stan invents a secret with the view to extracting a real secret from Simon. Stan says, 'I want to tell you something about my company that's really frustrating. It's all hush-hush, but it's just so stupid. You understand the pharmaceuticals industry so you'll really understand this, but can you please keep it just between us?'

Simon says, 'Yeah, sure.'

Stan asked permission and now Simon has responded positively and is committed to learning a secret about the other company; Simon has bought into the process. Psychologically, this strengthens Simon's obligation to return with the same sort of information and a secret relationship is now forming.

Stan says, 'Well, please don't tell anyone, but we have cut 30% from our research and development budget and stopped our research into the new migraine medication.'

Simon says, 'Yeah, that seems crazy, but I read an email from the boss the other day that said we were going to reduce our research and development budget and divert the funds toward importing precursors from China to minimise production costs here.'

Stan says, 'Really? How would that impact on you?'

Simon says, 'Well, I should be okay because as you know I'm in sales and the company needs more sales as we're slowly losing our market share.'

Stan says, 'Oh that's good, Simon—as long as you're all right. We can keep getting free conference lunches!'

Stan uses the divert technique of the READ Model (explained in Part Four) to move away from the secret subject area to a more positive subject, so the sharing fades from Simon's conscious mind and he feels positive, not regretful about the 'sharing' conversation.

Simon has unknowingly shared some very vital information to a competitor company. Why? Simon felt safe because of the environment he was in. Had this conversation occurred at the conference or in front of other employees, Simon would have been psychologically reminded of his obligations and loyalty.

Additionally, Stan has shared a (false) secret about his company's research and development budget. This made Simon feel as if the relationship had progressed to the point of sharing confidential information and due to feeling the quid pro quo obligation, he returned in kind with equally confidential information. Also, as a secret relationship is forming between them and Simon has now 'shared' once, it is highly likely that Simon will continue to share sensitive information with Stan. In fact, Simon may even initiate contact with Stan so he can offload more information, as Stan is now his elicitation friend/confidante; such is the power of quid pro quo and effective elicitation.

Believe It: Disbelief Works!

Disbelief can be a useful tool for eliciting additional details from a secret-keeper when the person has already shared some information. This requires you to, in a non-aggressive way, disbelieve the secret-keeper so the person feels the need to qualify or prove the correctness of the statement. To continue on with the example from the previous section:

Simon says, 'Well, I should be okay because as you know I'm in sales and the company needs more sales as we're slowly losing our market share.'

Stan says, 'No way, really? I've seen the promotional stuff you've been handing out at the conference; it's better quality than ours. It doesn't look like you guys are struggling to make money!'

Simon says, 'Yeah, it's true. In fact, to keep it all under the radar, we've been cutting back on all our internal costs so we can afford more marketing because we need customers. Even one of the bosses has lost his company car. I don't think any of us will be getting a bonus this year.'

By using disbelief Stan's was able to elicit additional details from Simon. If Stan's company was considering expanding via a hostile takeover Simon's company would be right in the crosshairs!

Disbelief can be used in many different industries and situations.

Disbelief has its uses

- Workplace investigators, police and lawyers may 'disbelieve' a witness or a confessing suspect to seek additional corroboration of any admission, additional information or circumstances, e.g. 'It's true; I saw it. You can even speak to my neighbor because she saw the same thing.'

- Medical staff may 'disbelieve' a patient to elicit additional details about a medical history. 'Yes, I've been prescribed these before; you can phone Dr Wynne at his practice.'

- Teachers may 'disbelieve' a student who tells them that the normally good student was to blame for the incident; to evoke a more detailed account of the event.

- Negotiators may 'disbelieve' an offer from the other side by disputing their capacity to deliver what was offered.

The use of disbelief is widely applicable when a secret-keeper has shared some but not all of their information and you want to corroborate its accuracy or seek additional information.

False Statement

The use of a false statement works similarly to disbelief. It requires you to deliberately state something that is incorrect in front of the secret-keeper, who will then correct what you have said and, in doing so, provide you with information. This elicitation line works particularly well on egocentric people, self-important people, technically minded people (who usually find it hard to tolerate inaccuracies), and often people in senior corporate positions. It's also a difficult line to cast if you fit into one of these categories yourself, as you will need to 'play the fool' to a certain degree, or at least feign ignorance or naivety.

Years ago, Peter Falk played a television character called Columbo who was a detective who used this technique to good effect. Often he was quite prepared to play the vague and haphazard investigator, by drawing the wrong conclusions or making incorrect assumptions in front of witnesses and suspects who couldn't help but correct the blundering old man. In doing so he elicited a great deal of information from these helpful secret-keepers and employed his Sherlock Holmesian powers of deduction to put the bad guy away every week—in fact, week after week for years! Even though this was fiction the same human response to an incorrect statement depicted was very real.

Using false statements to your advantage

You want to purchase another car and by co-incidence you meet a senior manager from your local car dealer at a party. He will have valuable hidden information that will assist you—he's now the secret-keeper. You are interested in purchasing a car but you can't really afford to pay the full price of a new car, or you don't want to! So you take this opportunity to gain hidden information from this secret-keeper about pricing.

After using your hook to start the conversation flowing you tell the manager that it must be hard in today's market as car retailers only make 1%–2% on each vehicle (knowing the net profit is more like 5%–10%) so it must be almost impossible to make a living.

The manager then tells you that's not correct; it's more like 5% and there are also some great incentives for dealerships that sell the new sports model, so he has ordered an additional amount. You then use another false statement and say that surely because the dollar has decreased in value and those models are imported they would be more expensive than ever and that would cut into the profit margin. He then corrects you and says that the cars he is getting landed in the country before the dollar value decreased, so he's getting them cheaper than other dealers who ordered them later. He says he's lucky because there'll be a national marketing campaign advertising them based on the increased dollar price, so he'll make at least 10% per unit, not 5% like the others.

By using false statements you were able to learn a great deal about where you could buy a new car from a dealer who is positioned to make an increased profit margin. Knowing this, you would then be able to carry out a robust negotiation with that dealership and likely purchase the car cheaper than at any other dealership.

When you use a deliberately false statement it's okay to misunderstand or not know something, but it's important that you don't say something that is so incorrect or naive that it impacts negatively on your credibility in the eyes of the secret-keeper. This may prevent the secret-keeper from sharing secret information with you. To circumvent this you can introduce a fictional third party so you can defer the incorrect information, assessment or statement to that person, e.g. 'I was told by a friend of mine who said ...' or, 'I read on an industry blog that ...' This will protect your credibility yet still deliver the same outcome.

The elicitation line of a false statement can work very well as a complementary strategy to other lines, as long as your credibility is not tarnished due to an overuse of naivety.

I'll Never See You Again

We know that it is rare for a person to keep a secret and that the natural urge to divulge a secret is the human default position. As such, most secret-keepers tell at least one other person their secret. We also learned in *Part One* that the majority of research on why we keep secrets has found that we want to avoid detrimental social consequences to ourselves or others. In fact, one study showed that 92.8% of reasons for keeping a secret was to protect the secret-keeper and his/her relationships from negative social consequences.[72] This places secret-keepers in a position of balancing the natural urge to share against the potential detrimental consequences of sharing.

One way for a secret-keeper to share information with the reduced risk of consequences is in a one-off meeting with a person who they'll never see again.

This situation allows a secret-keeper to lighten the psychological load by sharing the secret, with little or no chance of any detrimental social consequences. This type of situation may occur at an interstate conference, on a plane, train or bus or at a rare social or business engagement. If you are in a situation where you will only interact with a secret-keeper once, it's worth reinforcing the fact that you will never see each other again. The secret-keeper will self-assess the reduced consequences of sharing secret information with you in that situation. However, you may also choose to verbalize that your joint situation presents a unique opportunity to share confidential information and gain each other's views without the risk of others finding out.

One-off meetings

You're at a party away from your home town, or the secret-keeper is at the party and visiting from elsewhere, and you discover this person has some hidden information you would like to know. In this situation, it would be worthwhile telling the secret-keeper that because you'll never see each other again, you would like to share a secret. Then share a real or fabricated secret. The fact that you have shared a secret will create feelings of interrelatedness and your statement will cause the person to reflect on their own situation and the opportunity to do the same, i.e. 'I will never see this person again, so I can offload my secret harmlessly.' This way the secret-keeper will feel freer to share closely held information.

An opportunity such as this is not always used for self-serving purposes. It is also a fantastic opportunity to providing some much needed insight and support for the secret-keeper by providing some external perspective on the hidden information. As such, you may simply use the situation and your elicitation techniques to assist a person (who you'll only meet once) who is carrying a burdensome secret.

Pick a Common Enemy

If you support a particular sports team and you go to the game dressed in the team's colors and sit next to a similarly clad supporter, you will enjoy the feeling of common purpose. This occurs without a word being spoken. You are both on the same side and the desire to beat the other team is something you share. If one of the opposing team's supporters sat in front of the two of you, this would likely increase the feeling of kinship between you. If the opposing supporter then blew up a large inflatable hand (in the colors of the opposing team) and waved it around partially blocking your view of the match, the feeling of kinship would intensify considerably. So would your joint disapproval of the opposing supporter. If the other supporter of your team leaned over to you and said (about the waving hand), 'That's so rude. I can barely see what's going on!,' you would probably acknowledge and agree with the comment. If the other supporter told the opposing supporter to deflate the hand, you may even supportively contribute to that exchange. You both have a common enemy.

In a different context, imagine you were waiting in line at the check-in desk of an airport and there was an announcement that your flight was to be delayed by two hours and the person next to you said, 'Can you believe this? The flight is going to be at least two hours late, and last time they said that it was actually an hour longer.' You may be inclined to agree or to offer a similarly critical comment on the airline and highlight your common purpose against an adversary.

The adage 'the enemy of my enemy is my friend' is applicable to elicitation. It immediately puts you on the same side and you share the same feelings about the same issue at the same time. This, as you may recall from our earlier discussion, creates an emotional link, which assists with the flow of information between two people. Surprisingly, this type of bond is stronger when two people are faced with a common adversary; more so than when two individuals simply agree and like the same thing.

Taking sides

If a secret-keeper expresses their like for a particular singer, agreeing with them helps to build rapport because you have something in common, but not as strongly as if the secret-keeper expressed how intensely s/he didn't like that singer and you agreed with that sentiment. If you are in a situation where a secret-keeper expresses discontent/dislike about an issue, agreeing with the person will show emotional empathy and result in closer rapport.

Interestingly, there is a body of research that shows that anger empowers people as it washes away barriers that may impede actions or prevents information flow in the absence of anger. You certainly don't want the secret-keeper to be angry at you—*but* angry with you against others can be a uniting experience and form a bond of considerable strength.

If the secret-keeper was expressing a dislike for a particular function or part of a company, you would do well to allow the person to vent some anger and frustration to you, support those sentiments and psychologically mirror the secret-keeper. This will be cathartic for the secret-keeper and psychologically bring you closer, and at that point the barrier that is usually in place to protect hidden information is lowered. However, a secret-keeper that gets too irate may then associate you with those emotions when next you meet. So if the person appears to be getting a bit too emotional, calm the person and divert the conversation to a more positive subject area.

During your conversation, look for people, places or things that the secret-keeper has strong negative feelings about as the more intense their emotions, the closer the person will feel to you when you concur with their view.

This elicitation technique is rarely adequate by itself, but when used in conjunction with additional elicitation lines it can add a definite edge to your efforts.

Exclusively Yours!

We humans are quite hard to fathom sometimes. When there are things in plentiful supply, we don't have the dire urge to have whatever it is. However, when it's exclusive, scarce or in short supply, we want it. We really, really want it.

The more exclusive something becomes the higher value people place on it. For example, replica Elvis Presley concert posters that are printed in their thousands are considered worthless by collectors. But they'll pay a significant amount for an original poster, more for an original signed poster and a small fortune for the last poster ever signed by Elvis. We seem to equate rarity with value. The less there is of something the more valuable it is to us.

I want it because I can't have it

The incandescent light bulb has been around in various forms since the 19th century. Over several decades the sales of these light bulbs have remained stable with little to upset market. These functional but uninspiring bulbs were in plentiful supply, were cheap and readily available. But in 2005 things were about to change. Various countries commenced planning to phase out the incandescent light bulb and replace it with compact fluorescent lamps (CFL) or LED lamps to minimise economic and environmental costs.

When it was announced in Germany that the incandescent light bulb would be banned, sales increased by 34%.[73] This market spike has been replicated in most countries in response to such announcements, showing the highest ever increase in sales for the soon to be rare light bulb. When it became known that these bulbs would no longer be so plentiful, people wanted them more than ever, even though there was a suitable replacement and there would be no shortage of CFL light bulbs in future.

Similarly in the 1980s, due to a falling market share the Coca-Cola Company conducted an extensive development and market research program to develop a new Coke formula, including 200,000 taste tests. According to the tests, 55% preferred the 'new' Coke over the original version. Most of the tests were conducted blindfolded; however, when participants were told which one was the new Coke the satisfaction rate increased to 61%!

Coke executives must have been very excited by the test results that showed most preferred the 'new' formula and assumed this additional 6% was the result of the participants wanting a change from the old. They were wrong! Critically, this had been misinterpreted; what they were actually witnessing was the participants wanting the yet-to-be released and at that time very exclusive Coke. The additional 6% was not the want of something new, but a desire to have what was scarce and exclusive.

Consistent with the scarce and exclusive principle, when the 'new' Coke hit the shelves in 1985, sales initially increased by 8% as the 'new' Coke was still relatively new and rare. However, as the 'new' Coke flooded the market, sales plummeted and protests increased. People even started hoarding the original Coke, as it was slowly being replaced on shelves; it was becoming rare. Now the original Coke, the one with the previously dwindling market share, was the Coke that people could no longer have, and as a consequence, it became their favorite. There was such a significant backlash that on 10 July 1985, less than three months after the 'new' Coke was released, it was announced that original Coke would be returned to the shelves.

The drive people have when they feel they may miss out or only have a limited chance to gain a rare opportunity is both competitive and compelling and as such, this aspect of human nature is targeted by advertisers. Clever marketing teams behind successful acts promote 'for one night only' or the 'farewell tour' to emphasise that there is a dwindling chance to see a particular act. This desire to have what is scarce is not limited to collectors' items and the rich and famous. Consider the crowds that line up outside stores when there is an annual or a closing down sale, usually accompanied by advertising such as, 'Hurry in! The sale ends tomorrow' or 'Last chance to get a bargain'.

The reason for these all too common sales pitches is that they work and they continue to work on the human psyche. When something is promoted as 'limited edition' or 'for a short time only,' regardless of whether it's cars, coins, stamps, shirts, prints, even a type of burger or drink, it boosts sales. It's in short supply so people want it more.

Can this also apply to information? Do people also crave rare and exclusive information? Yes they do, and one study highlights this point particularly well. When wholesale beef buyers in the US were informed that adverse Australian weather conditions may reduce the amount of available Australian beef, orders were doubled.[74] But when the wholesalers were informed the information came from an exclusive source, sales increased by 600%![75]

Similarly, supposed 'insider information' about a company or even a currency that finds its way to the stock market has been shown to have an impact on stock prices. For most people, if the information is exclusive or not known by many it carries with it instant credibility and it becomes compelling information.

Just like rare opportunities and exclusive things that people want when they are in short supply, the more exclusive the information the more influential it can be. We can use this when interacting with secret-keepers by pointing out how exclusive the relationship is: 'We are so lucky to have a relationship of trust where we can share information with each other—relationships like this are rare.'

Additionally when sharing a secret with a secret-keeper in order to have that person reciprocate with their own secret information, it will serve you well to point out how exclusive your information is.

In fact, a strategy of telling the secret-keeper that you want to divulge something that you have never told anybody before, but you are not sure whether you should share the information or not, will have the secret-keeper really wanting to know what the information is . It's information that would be exclusively theirs if they can just obtain it from you.

After you have shared the information, reinforce how exclusive it is, then rely on quid pro quo to elicit similarly exclusive, hidden information from the secret-keeper. Similar strategies may be helpful when providing support, counselling and advice to secret-keepers; for example, by reinforcing how unique the relationship is and that the information shared between you is exclusive to that very relationship.

Gee, You Really are Important; Please Tell Me More!

If there is an ideal secret-keeper to elicit information from it's a person who feels the need to impress others. Eliciting information from this type of person is like taking candy from a baby—which isn't a valid elicitation goal! By asking simple questions, we can provoke this type of person to impress us with knowledge. To do this you can position yourself as being very interested, keen to learn and almost in awe of the person's knowledge during the general conversation and gradually steer the conversation to the secret area.

When the conversation arrives at that sensitive place it becomes difficult for the person to suddenly transform from the expert who is leading the conversation to a defensive and reserved character. These people simply love the sound of their own voice and being centre stage. Once you get the person talking (which isn't usually very hard), they find it hard to hand the microphone over to someone else when the conversation arrives at a secret subject area.

The opportunity to impress simply impairs the person's judgement so much so that feelings of their own or others privacy, company loyalty and confidentiality pale into insignificance. Keep them talking (and impressing you!) with: 'I never knew that!,' 'That's amazing!,' 'Is there more, or is that all you know?'

To access further information, you may even ask the secret-keeper a hypothetical question that you (pretend) to find complex or interesting and seek the person's advice or insight. For example, 'So if your company was to ...' or 'If your CEO was suddenly taken ill and you took over, what changes would you make?,' or 'You may not be able to help but I was wondering if a new investor came along ...' These types of questions will have the 'oracle' sharing some much valued insight into the inner workings of a company. The same strategy may be applied to any secret-keeper who feels the need to impress.

Professionals, researchers, technical people and senior managers, who all have access to sensitive information, may be vulnerable to the 'Gee, you really are important!' line when their ego is not in check.

Selecting a Syncher

So you've used an excellent elicitation hook and the secret-keeper was immediately drawn into your conversation. You've cast a few elicitation lines (flattery, quid pro quo, etc.) and as a result you and the secret-keeper now share a solid rapport, the secret-keeper has commenced opening up to you and is sharing information. The next time you meet the secret-keeper you don't want to have to start at the beginning again and commence re-establishing your rapport with the person. So now you start looking for synchers. It's a bad pun I know (sorry), but its purpose is simple—to SYNCHronise the positive feelings and close rapport from one conversation to a new conversation.

It's ideal to commence your next conversation in exactly the same way you ended the previous conversation, so that interaction starts as positively and warmly as the first one ended. To do this we want to reaffirm the interpersonal platform of sharing by reigniting the positive aspects from the first interaction. In other words we want to be able to prompt the secret-keeper to recall the positive and/

or close emotional 'feelings' from the previous encounter. To do this, as you are talking with the secret-keeper during the first conversation, look for parts of the conversation when the person acts very positively or reacts by suddenly sharing information—these are Synchers.

Synchers stand out during a conversation as the secret-keeper will react happily and/or start to share information that is more intimate than all previous information offered during the conversation. Whatever triggered that reaction is a syncher to use next time you meet.

Synchers may occur during a conversation in response to:

- Something you say, or
- Something the secret-keeper says.

If for some reason you had a conversation and the person mentioned that their pet had recently died and the person became emotional, would you raise that subject again? Of course not, as it would be likely to once again upset the person. This is a negative syncher.

The same principle applies to positive synchers. It's the positive ones that you want to select from the first conversation to use in the second conversation. You want to select parts of the first conversation where you were particularly close and replicate that in the psyche of the secret-keeper early during the second conversation. This should synchronise you both immediately to the closeness of the first conversation.

Synchronising with someone

Consider that during your conversation you mention Jerry Seinfeld and what a funny comedian he is and the secret-keeper reacts by smiling then proceeding to tell you that he has seen all the episodes; that is a syncher. If the circumstances allow, you can gain an even more effective syncher by asking what episode the person thought was funniest and discussing that. If, for example, the person mentions a funny line or part of the episode that gives you an even better syncher, as this is something very positive in the secret-keeper's mind.

Perhaps the secret-keeper tells you how funny it is when Jerry says, 'Hi, Newman' in a despising tone to the rotund postman. This is an excellent syncher. When you next meet, you may even say 'Hi, Newman' to the secret-keeper to reignite the person's happy emotions about that episode; critically, this also reignites the same feelings you share about the same thing. This will reinforce the emotional link from the previous conversation. It will put you in synch.

While it's usually ideal, the syncher need not always be a purely happy one; it just has to be something in the conversation that caused you both to share closely held information.

For example, you mention that your supervisor was very supportive. The secret-keeper responded by telling you that his supervisor was very unappreciative of him then started to share details about activities in the workplace; the syncher is the secret-keeper's supervisor. Next time you meet, using psychological mirroring and dropping a syncher should take you both straight to the previous sharing state. For example, you may use this syncher: 'My supervisor isn't as supportive of me as she used to be; in fact, she barely notices how much work I do these days.' This should immediately initiate the secret-keeper talking about his supervisor and details about the workplace.

The subject of the syncher does not need to be the actual subject matter that you are seeking details about, just one where sharing more intimate information than normal occurred.

If the secret-keeper starts to talk fondly about family then go with that and share some similar family stories. Any sharing is good sharing. Then during the conversation, you can direct the conversation toward the hidden information. But remember that the syncher in that instance is family, so when you meet again drop that syncher by talking about your family. This will take you both to a sharing platform and you can circumvent all the work you previously invested to get to the same point in the first meeting.

Refer to the section 'Psychological mirroring: Two mirrors in a lift' in *Part 2* to see an example of an effective syncher.

Whenever you notice a secret-keeper react positively or suddenly start to share information, take note of what caused that, and keep that syncher to use in a later conversation. When you next meet, this will return you immediately to the close sharing precedence of the previous conversation.

PART THREE KEY POINTS

- An 'elicitation hook' is a conversational technique used to immediately hook the secret-keeper into a conversation.

- There are two critical elements of an elicitation hook:

  1. Statement: The statement part of the hook should be a mutual point of interest; a point of commonality that you and the secret-keeper both share or agree upon.

  2. Question: The question component should cause the secret-keeper to talk with you.

- An 'elicitation line' is a technique or strategy used to influence a secret-keeper to open up (beyond the hook) and talk with you.

- When using elicitation lines it's critical that the secret-keeper believes you are sincere. The fastest way an emotional link is broken is when the secret-keeper believes you are being insincere.

- Some of the most successful elicitation techniques include:

  - Flattery

  - Sharing a secret secret to uncover a real secret

  - Quid pro quo—reciprocity

  - Disbelief

  - False statement

  - I'll never see you again

  - Pick a common enemy

  - Exclusively yours!

  - Gee, you really are important—please tell me more!

- Flattery should be used sparingly as people are very adept at identifying false compliments. The flattery elicitation line is most effective when it's delivered subtly and where possible, via a third party the secret-keeper identifies with.

- Never share a secret with secret-keepers about another person, as it may cause them to reflect upon whether you can keep their information secret.

- If you want to reinforce just how confidential you keep information without saying 'trust me' (as this never works!), try, 'Well, someone told me something confidential about that, but I can't talk about it because I said I wouldn't tell anyone.' This is far more effective as the secret-keeper will use statements like this as a benchmark when measuring your trustworthiness and assessing whether to trust sharing information with you.

- The fastest way to ignite a new relationship and build rapport with a person is to add the ingredient of secrecy to the relationship. Sharing an exclusive secret can amplify attraction between two people.

- The purpose of a syncher is to SYNCHronise the positive feelings and close rapport from one conversation to a later conversation.

- Synchers stand out during a conversation as the secret-keeper will react happily and/or start to share information that is more intimate than all previous information during the conversation. Whatever triggered that reaction is a syncher to use next time you meet.

PUTTING IT ALL TOGETHER:
Unlocking Secrets to Solve a True Crime

The following example comes from a true undercover crime investigation into serial killer Robert William Pickton, following his arrest outside Vancouver on 5 February 2002. The details of this investiation were supressed for many years. However, I am now able to release this detailed account of how an undercover officer was able to unlock the very dangerous secrets from the mind of a serial killer. When you read through this example, you will notice some of the elicitation techniques we have discussed being used subtly and effectively. You now have the opportunity to see firsthand just how very effective these techniques can be; even with a person, who until then had locked his secret activities away from every person he knew. The techniques are so effective that they influence Pickton to share his greatest secrets with a total stranger.

Please be warned that this real crime example does contain some offensive language.

Vancouver, Canada. 5 February 2002

During the day, the Royal Canadian Mounted Police (RCMP) had received information that Robert William Pickton had illegal firearms on his ramshackle pig farm in Port Coquitlam, about 30 minutes drive from Vancouver's CBD.[76]

About 8.30 pm on that cold night, a small team of RCMP officers armed with a search warrant for illegal firearms crept onto Pickton's farm. At 8.35, five Entry Team officers smashed open the front door of the dilapidated building and arrested Pickton. Pickton was then taken to the police station as the search commenced. Illegal firearms were found almost immediately, but there was a lot more to be found on Pickton's pig farm ...

In one room an officer found a birth certificate in the name of Heather Bottomley. A short time later, another officer who was searching Pickton's office area opened a grey ski bag which had a number of items, including a pair of women's joggers and an asthma inhaler with the patient's name, Sereena Abotsway, typed on the label.

Both these women had previously been reported missing from Vancouver's Eastside area, dubbed 'skid row,' where drugs, prostitution, robbery and violence prevailed. These two names were part of a long list of women missing from that area. In fact, over the years female sex workers had been disappearing at such an alarming rate that a special joint police taskforce, the British Columbia Missing Women Investigation, was formed. The investigation had not identified the offender or offenders responsible, though there was a high degree of intelligence indicating that a serial killer was preying on skid row sex workers.

The day after the search warrant on Pictkon's farm (6 February 2002) about 16 hours after his arrest, Pickton was charged with firearms offences and released on bail. However, he was not allowed back on his farm as the RCMP were still searching the property; now under a different warrant—one relating to the long list of missing women. The press latched on to the story, and the farm, still guarded by the RCPM, was surrounded by television crews and reporters.

Sixteen days later on 22 February 2002, Pickton was arrested and formally charged with the murders of two missing woman. While he denied any involvement, police suspected Pickton was responsible for much more than just two murders.

After being charged Pickton was walked to the cell block by the guards. He was now aged 51, unshaven and was almost totally bald except for long, dirty, scraggly brown hair that hung from the very back of his head. Pickton was filthy and smelly but had refused the police offer to take a shower. The police then took his clothing and dressed him in a fresh white T-shirt and grey fleecy tracksuit and marched him towards his cell.

The cream-colored cell was about three metres square, the u-shaped cement bench along its three sides formed two beds and included a basic toilet and sink. The remaining side had the cell door which opened to a hallway. As Pickton was escorted along the hallway by the guards, he saw his cellmate was to be a large rough-looking career criminal who immediately shouted angrily at the guards that he wanted to see his lawyer and abused them for putting another person in his cell. Pickton entered the cell and sat quietly on the vacant bed. What he didn't know was that his aggressive cell mate was in fact an RCMP undercover officer …

I have worked and trained with RCMP undercover officers in Canada and they are, in my opinion, some of the best covert operatives in the world. The identity of this operative has necessarily been removed from the below transcript. However,

I can tell you that he had very little warning or information about his sudden covert deployment and its requirements. All he was told was that he was to share a cell with a 51-year-old suspect who had been arrested on two counts of murder. Additionally, he was shown Pickton's murder charge sheet.[77] Without the benefit of a significant research phase (see *Part Four*), the operative had to rely purely upon his indirect elicitation skills (the same as we have discussed in *Parts Two* and *Three*) to see if Pickton would share his hidden information with him, and the recording devices and camera hidden in the cell.

Below I have listed several excerpts of the recorded conversations that took place over three days following Pickton's arrest.[78] As this is actual transcript from a real police undercover operation there are, as is usually the case, several parts of the conversation that are inaudible due to technical difficulties or crosstalk. As such there are gaps in the conversation. However, the above background story should assist you in understanding the context of the conversations.

As you read the excerpts you will notice that as a result of the operative's clever indirect elicitation techniques and successful psychological mirroring, Pickton's relationship with the operative changes. It transforms from that of two strangers, where Pickton hides information and denies any involvement in the murders; to two confidantes, where Picton shares that he killed 49 women and how he disposed of some of the bodies. The operative successfully becomes 'that person' to Pickton.

Please be advised: These undercover excerpts contain offensive language.

Excerpt One

Psychological Mirroring and Elicitation Line 'Pick a Common Enemy'

Robert Pickton: He says that they are gonna charge me for murder one on two counts.

Undercover officer: Hum. Fuck. That's fuckin' pretty heavy shit, there.

Robert Pickton: You know what? Sometimes innocent people go to jail too.

Undercover officer: Sometimes? Tell me about it. You know what? They gotta fuckin' prove it first. Yeah, I'll tell ya that too.

Robert Pickton: What's that?

Undercover officer: They gotta fuckin' prove it too.

Robert Pickton: No they don't have to prove anything. They don't have to prove nothing.

Undercover officer: What'll they do? They can't fuckin' keep you here if they got nothing on you, I'll tell you that, man.

Robert Pickton: They can set you up. They can set you up.

Undercover officer: Do you think?

Robert Pickton: Fuckin' right. These are cops and they're dirty at that.

Undercover officer: Can't trust a cop, man; believe that.

Robert Pickton: These are fuckin' cops and you can't trust the fuckin' cocksuckers.

Undercover officer: Yeah, you're right there. You're fuckin' eh, you're right on the money on that one.

Robert Pickton: They is, they could, document anything at all.

Undercover officer: Well they'll try anyway. Fuckin' try.

Robert Pickton: Well, they can. They got me up for ah, murder one, two counts.

Undercover officer: Hm.

Robert Pickton: And I don't know nothing about it.

Excerpt Two

Psychological Mirroring and Elicitation Lines 'Disbelief' and 'Flattery'

Robert Pickton: I'm a plain old pig farmer. (Nodding)

Undercover officer: Pig farmer? So you're that fuckin' guy that ah... (*refers to media reports*). Yeah, sure you are. You don't look like no fuckin' pig farmer to me …

Robert Pickton: So I go to work then and (indecipherable) … all of sudden then, they got my gun, now I'm in jail.

Undercover officer: That's, that's not right.

Robert Pickton: Now they're trying to charge me for 50 murders. Fifty fuckin' murders. Fuck off.

Undercover officer: They're fucked; they can't.

Robert Pickton: Fifty fuckin' murders, me?

Undercover officer: Yeah that's… I still don't fucken believe ya.

Robert Pickton: Huh?

Undercover officer: Fuckin' I still don't believe that. I think you're fuckin' bull shittin' me. Like I said, just look atcha.

Excerpt Three

Elicitation Lines 'Flattery' and 'Gee, You're Really Important— Tell Me More'

Robert Pickton: The whole fuckin' world knows me. All the way to Hong Kong to everywhere. Even Hong Kong.

Undercover officer: Fuck. I never knew you're world renowned.

Robert Pickton: What's that?

Undercover officer: You're an all-star. Fuck, it's not that big.

Robert Pickton: All the way to Hong Kong.

Undercover officer: Fuck, the next think you'll be like King Tut or Saddam Hussein and those guys.

Robert Pickton: Kinda nice to be similar to Saddam …

Excerpt Four

*Emphasising Similarities and Elicitation Line 'Sharing a
Secret Secret to Uncover a Real Secret'*

Robert Pickton: So what are you in here for?

Undercover officer: You really want to know? What do you want to know? Ah, between me and you, I'm fuckin' wanted for some pretty heavy shit back east.

Robert Pickton: Just ah, about breach warrants?

Undercover officer: I don't … no fuck those warrants. Fuck, it's the bad stuff.

Robert Pickton: What's that?

Undercover officer: Take a guess. What are you sittin' in here for?

Robert Pickton: I got ah, two attempt murder charges, ah, two murder charges against me.

Undercover officer: Yeah. I'm going down, fuckin' ah, fuckin' attempt …

Robert Pickton: Attempt murder?

Undercover officer: Yeah, back east.

Excerpt Five

Elicitation Line 'Quid Pro Quo—Reciprocity'

(The meals have just been delivered to the cell with cups of coffee. The undercover officer does Pickton a favor. Without being able to repay the favor in a similar way, information is later given up by Pickton)

Undercover officer: What is it? *(referring to the meal)*

Robert Pickton: I don't know.

Undercover officer: Fuckin' beans or somethin'.

Robert Pickton: This (indecipherable). Aw, coffee!

Undercover officer: You don't drink coffee?

Robert Pickton: No.

Undercover officer: Really?

Robert Pickton: No.

Undercover officer: Why don't you tell 'em you want juice or something? They'll get some.

(Minutes later)

Undercover officer: Guard! Can you get juice or water or something else?

Guard: No, there's water in the tap there ... Okay, might have some juice.

Undercover officer: Can you get a cup or something?

Robert Pickton: I don't drink coffee.

Undercover officer: He doesn't like coffee.

Guard: Doesn't drink coffee?

Undercover officer: No.

Guard: Okay, I'll see if I can find some juice.

Excerpt Six

Excellent Psychological Mirroring and Elicitation Line 'Flattery'

(The operative picks up the respect Pickton has for his brother and psychologically mirrors Pickton, creating a strong psychological link)

Undercover officer: Yeah, but you gotta fuckin' cover your own ass I'm telling you.

Robert Pickton: That's what my brother said to me.

Undercover officer: You think those fuckin' guys are gonna care about your ass?

Robert Pickton: That's what my brother was worried about.

Undercover officer: Well, it sounds like your brother's a pretty smart guy; he's been around a lot.

Robert Pickton: Yup.

Undercover officer: He knows how business is done.

Robert Pickton: He warned me I'm screwed.

Undercover officer: Well, you should have fuckin' took a plane down to fuckin' Cuba somewhere.

Robert Pickton: I'm just a plain pig farmer.

Undercover officer: Not anymore, my friend.

Robert Pickton: The whole world knows me now.

Undercover officer: That's right; you're fuckin' ah, like a legend.

Robert Pickton: Really I am now. Doesn't matter where I go.

Excerpt Seven

Emphasising Similarities, Psychological Mirroring and Elicitation Line 'Flattery'

Undercover officer: You're a clean cut kinda guy, just a workin' joey.

Robert Pickton: It's all I am, just a farm boy.

Undercover officer: I know what farm work's like. I spent a few years on the farm myself.

(Break)

Undercover officer: Those are fun days.

Robert Pickton: Oh yeah.

Undercover officer: Growing up.

Robert Pickton: That's ah, when you're growing up.

Undercover officer: You gotta, especially farm kids eh?

Robert Pickton: Yeah. I mean ah … I stopped.

Undercover officer: We used to jump off the fuckin' bales into the big hay …

Robert Pickton: I worked hard all my life.

Undercover officer: You got to like, if you live on a farm.

Robert Pickton: Yeah.

Undercover officer: Haul water and …

Robert Pickton: Six-thirty in the morning, you're up.

Undercover officer: Yeah, chores.

Robert Pickton: Get up and get out there and milk the cows.

Undercover officer: Yeah.

Robert Pickton: Come back in, get cleaned up, and get ready for school.

Undercover officer: Yeah.

Robert Pickton: Come back from school, go out and milk the cows again.

Undercover officer: Yeah. That's right. Fuckin' feed 'em, water 'em.

(Break)

Robert Pickton: So, so hard.

Undercover officer: That's the kind of … you worked hard, you're right you know. That's how you pay your way, that's how you made a success, where you fuckin' got money from.

Robert Pickton: Now I'm up for murder, I'll lose everything.

Undercover officer: Doesn't seem fair.

Robert Pickton: I lose everything. I lose everything, everything I worked for.

Undercover officer: But they can't take the fuckin' hard work from you, though.

Robert Pickton: But, I'd still do it tomorrow, the same thing, help people, everything else.

Undercover officer: Don't let it change ya.

Robert Pickton: Hum?

Undercover officer: Yeah, don't let it change you, be who you are.

Robert Pickton: Yeah. I won't change myself much. I won't change myself very much.

Undercover officer: Yeah. Well sounds like you led a fuckin' good life though, like you said.

Excerpt Eight

Elicitation Lines 'Sharing a Secret Secret to Uncover a Real Secret' and Quid Pro Quo—Reciprocity

(By sharing a fabricated secret, the operative induces Pickton to share similar information to repay the obligation. From this point Pickton increases how much information he is prepared to share; he confesses how he disposed of some of the bodies and to killing 49 people)

Undercover officer: Fuckin' a guy does it right. I find the best way to fuckin' dispose of something *(referring to a body)* is fuckin' take it to the ocean.

Robert Pickton: Oh, really?

Undercover officer: Oh, fuck, do you know what the fuckin' ocean does to things? There ain't much left.

Robert Pickton: I did better than that.

Undercover officer: Who?

Robert Pickton: Me.

Undercover officer: No. Huh.

(Pickton gets up and sits close to the operative)

Robert Pickton: A rendering plant.

Undercover officer: Hey?

Robert Pickton: A rendering plant.

Undercover officer: Ha, ha. No shit. Ha, ha, that's gotta be fuckin' ah, pretty good hey.

Robert Pickton: Mm, hmm.

Undercover officer: Can't be much fuckin' left?

Robert Pickton: Oh, no only ah, I was kinda sloppy at the end, too, getting too sloppy.

Undercover officer: Really.

Robert Pickton: They got me, oh, fuck, gettin' too sloppy.

Undercover officer: See, fuck, you gotta be fuckin' meticulous you gotta be ...

Robert Pickton: (Indecipherable).

Undercover officer: That's pretty, that's fuckin' pretty ... pretty good man.

Robert Pickton: Mmm?

Undercover officer: That's fuckin' pretty good. You must be doing something right, Ha, ha. Fuckin' beautiful ...

(Break)

Robert Pickton: I was gonna do one more, make it an even fifty.

Undercover officer: (Laughing)

Robert Pickton: That's why, that's why I was sloppy about (indecipherable).

Undercover officer: Yeah.

Robert Pickton: I wanted one more, make, make the big five O.

Undercover officer: Make the big five zero (Laughing). Fuck. That's fucked, Fuckin' five zero. Fuckin' half a hundred.

(Pickton laughing, nodding)

Robert Pickton: Mmm Hmm.

Robert Pickton: Everybody says, how many of those *(bodies)*? I wouldn't tell 'em.

Excerpt Nine

Elicitation Line 'Gee You're Really Important—Please Tell Me More'

Robert Pickton: Really fuckin' pisses me off. I was just gonna fuckin' do one more make it even.

Undercover officer: (Laughing)

Robert Pickton: Bigger than the, bigger than the ones in the States.

(Referring to US serial killers, in particular serial killer Gary Leon Ridgway, the 'Green River Killer,' who was arrested the year before.)

Undercover officer: Yeah. Oh yeah, fuckin' by far.

Robert Pickton: His record was about 42 they says.

Undercover officer: Yeah, is it.

Robert Pickton: Forty-two.

Undercover officer: Fuckin' it looks like you got the record.

Robert Pickton: This is big right now it's big, it's growing.

(Break)

Robert Pickton: Forty-nine!

Undercover officer: Almost made it.

Robert Pickton: Hum, almost made it.

Robert Pickton: I'm worried about it.

Undercover officer: Hee hee.

Robert Pickton: All the way up to 50.

Undercover officer: Hey?

Robert Pickton: I haven't done 50 yet.

Undercover officer: Yeah. Yeah ...

(Break)

Robert Pickton: I can't believe it I mean ...

Undercover officer: (Laughs) I can't believe it, I'm with the fuckin' Pigman! You'll be fuckin' signing autographs... Hmm.

Robert Pickton: That's big ... that's bigger than the ... Green River.

Undercover officer: Oh yeah, I don't know. What was that?

Robert Pickton: Forty-two.

Concluding Excerpt

Robert Pickton: So I'll see what's gonna happen tomorrow. Tomorrow's gonna be very interesting. My lawyer says don't say nothing.

Undercover officer: Perfect!

The Result

During his time with Pickton, the operative used six of the nine elicitation lines we discussed in *Part Three*. Additionally, the operative deliberately increased his 'likeability' and continually psychologically mirrored Pickton. Within a short time, an abhorrent and dangerous criminal, who had kept his killings secret for over a decade, was suddenly prepared to share his most hidden information with a stranger—such is the nature of effective elicitation.

As a result of the excellent elicitation skills of the operative, painstaking forensic crime scene processing and dedicated police work, Pickton was charged with 26 counts of murder. For legal reasons only six were proceeded with initially. In December 2007, Pickton was found guilty of second-degree murder on all six counts.[79] For those six murders, Pickton was sentenced to 25 years without parole; the maximum available for second-degree murder under Canadian law. The Crown prosecutor later decided it was not in the public interest to proceed with the remaining 20 first-degree murder charges.[80] The investigation and trial cost $102 million.[81]

R
E
A
D

Part Four:

The READ Model of Elicitation

So far we have discussed the nature of secrets, their impact and why people keep them. We have also learned some very clever conversational techniques to subtly encourage a secret-keeper to reveal their secret.

We have seen that these techniques can even be effective against very guarded and careful serial killers. However, elicitation, human dynamics and the psychology of secrets are individually complex subject areas and this book combines all three! As such, we need a clear and proven model to guide us through the otherwise complicated process. To answer that need, I developed the READ Model of Elicitation.

Practical Keys for Unlocking Secrets

Unlike the movies, spies and covert operatives don't simply walk up to a person they want information from and put a gun under their chin and threaten them, nor do they drug the person then photograph them in a compromising sexual encounter and blackmail them into giving information ... well, not that often! Regardless, these aren't tactics we can use as part of our day-to-day living. There are, however, more refined and more effective (and legal) methods that we can adapt to suit our purposes when we are seeking information. It is from these very complex and resource intensive operations that I have created an easy-to-follow and very effective elicitation template for everyday use, titled 'READ'. Before we have a look at that template, it's useful to have an understanding of the origins and the proving ground of the READ model; the shadowy world of espionage.

How Spies Use READ

After selecting the person who has access to the sought after secret information (the secret-keeper), covert operatives and their support teams spend many hundreds of hours profiling the secret-keeper well in advance to actually speaking with the person. Intelligence is gathered from every available avenue ranging from the person's phone usage, travel, spending habits and club memberships to personal and professional associations and sexual preferences. Every aspect of the person's life is examined. The purpose of this research or intelligence gathering phase is to develop a 'personality profile' that identifies the secret-keeper's likes, dislikes, strengths and weaknesses. This assists in determining a strategy on how best to approach the secret-keeper, what time such an approach should be made and, critically, what type of person is the best fit for eliciting information from that person. We discussed earlier (see 'Being That Person' in Part 2) that most secret-keepers tell at least one person their secret and in most cases it was a friend or confidante. All the research and intelligence gathering is aimed at engineering favorable circumstances and planning the meeting and the relationship so the covert operative can be 'that person'; the one the secret-keeper wants to share information with.

Making a match with a secret-keeper

The research phase revealed that a secret-keeper (usually referred to as the target) who had access to vital information was very fond of and bred Golden Retriever dogs. The secret-keeper was also very sympathetic to the plight of the Tibetan people. A suitable covert operative was then selected. Ideally this would have been a person of Tibetan ethnicity, or someone who may pass themself off as a Tibetan. However, there was no such operative available so a person who was very knowledgeable about Tibet and who could also be overtly sympathetic to the Tibetan cause was selected for the operation.

Well before the first meeting, the operative conducted extensive research into Golden Retriever dogs and even went to a number of dog shows. Surveillance had identified the secret-keeper's car keys had a Golden Retriever badge attached. This surveillance information provided the 'hook'. The operative psychologically mirrored the secret-keeper when they had their 'chance' meeting in an airport queue, and hooked the secret-keeper by 'noticing' the Golden Retriever badge. They immediately had a point of commonality and a 'natural' conversation about that breed ensued. As a result of some excellent planning, the secret-keeper and the operative were seated together during the flight and by casting some pre-planned elicitation lines a close rapport quickly developed. During the flight, the operative identified synchers that could be used when next they met.

This was the first of many well-planned elicitation engagements which from the secret-keeper's perspective were simply enjoyable social meetings. In a later meeting the operative divulged his secretly held 'Tibetan' sympathies and an emotional bond was struck (sharing a secret secret to reveal a real secret).

The secret-keeper then shared similarly held views and a relationship of mutual trust developed. The operative became 'that person' in the secret-keeper's life and could then set about eliciting the required information (over a series of meetings), without ever compromising the fact that the entire relationship had been engineered for a specific purpose.

This is a well used and trusted method used by intelligence agencies around the world for infiltration and elicitation.

As our elicitation isn't a matter of life and death or national security and we aren't infiltrating the KGB, we don't need to undertake a thorough and resource intensive operation. While we may not have surveillance teams, forensic accountants and psychological profilers to assist us, we can still adopt the same template for elicitation in our everyday lives. The READ model sets this out simply.

Spelling Out the READ Steps

READ is a handy acronym which sets out four easy steps to follow when you are attempting to unlock hidden information. It can be used for both long and short term elicitation and in both direct and indirect elicitation processes. Each step is as critical as the others and relies upon the previous one being undertaken. Regardless of the situation, to ensure your best chance of success, I recommend following this model.

R

Research and assess the secret-keeper.

- Research: Learn as much as possible about the secret-keeper. Depending on the circumstances, this may vary from a couple of minutes to a couple of months.

- Assess: Analyse the personality state of the secret-keeper in the environment when you are about to meet.

E

Engage the secret-keeper—hook, line and syncher.

- Hook: Based on your assessment, use psychological mirroring and an appropriate hook to initiate a conversation about a subject of mutual interest.

- Line: Then cast your elicitation line or lines to rapidly build rapport and bring you closer to the secret-keeper.

- Syncher: Take note of parts of the conversation that the secret-keeper reacts positively to, or suddenly starts sharing information about. These synchers can be used when next you meet, to recreate the secret-keeper's positive and/or close emotional 'feelings' from the previous encounter.

A

Access the hidden information—segue to secrecy: To subtly access the subject of the hidden information, during the conversation look for conversational gates or segues that you can use to steer the conversation to the secret subject area. Avoid asking direct questions as these are too stark, may spook the person and will definitely remain in the secret-keeper's mind well after the conversation. If you notice the secret-keeper starts to disengage from you or makes it clear that subject is off limits, continue to use elicitation lines and build rapport but move away from that subject area. However, if the information starts to flow learn as much as you can and set the stage for another meeting by taking note of synchers at this intimate sharing level.

D

Divert the conversation away from the sensitive subject area, so that the shared information is not prominent in the mind of the secret-keeper after the meeting has ended. Create a happy ending so the secret-keeper will be predisposed to commence your next meeting the same way.

Now we'll examine each step of the model in more detail to better understand how they fit together to form a very simple and effective elicitation strategy.

STEP ONE: Research and assess the secret-keeper

The more you know about a secret-keeper the better you will be able to tailor your engagement (the next step), this will in turn increase your chance of success. Regardless of whether you are simply eliciting information in a one-off chance meeting on a plane or at a cafe, spontaneously speaking with a client, patient or child, or alternatively undertaking a well-planned and complex elicitation strategy to gain vital investment information—the initial stage of research and assessment remains critical to your success. This will assist you to set an effective hook, cast elicitation lines that are likely to work favorably with the secret-keeper and rapidly build rapport when you first meet.

A research and assessment phase may only last a minute or two or take several weeks. Here is an example of a very quick research and assessment step that you could undertake when visiting an area where you plan to invest in property. There may be little point in asking the local real estate agents about such an idea (of course they will encourage you to buy!). One way to gain a good sense of the local area very quickly is to speak with some of the people who live there—in this situation they are the secret-keepers. You don't want to reveal that you are a potential house buyer or major investor in the local area, so you plan to elicit as much local information as possible.

As you walk into a cafe you quickly scan the body language of the customers and select a person (the secret-keeper) who appears to be in no hurry. This is critical, so you don't get brushed off by a busy person. Ideally you would also select a person who is dressed in a similar way to you, so the person feels at ease interacting with you.

Before approaching the secret-keeper, you need more information and you observe as much as you can, taking note of the type and quality of clothing the person is wearing. You pay particular attention to their shoes as these are often an underrated source of information. For example, a worn upper right toe may indicate the person rides a motorcycle (worn by constant gear changing), specks of paint may indicate a painter or home renovator, shabby high quality shoes may indicate a person is under some financial strain. By themselves shoes don't tell the whole picture about a person, but they can add some vital information to your complete assessment. (As long as the person hasn't borrowed someone's shoes!)

Your research continues and you look for more obvious clues such as a company name tag, club or souvenir motifs sewn into their shirt, engraving on a belt buckle or a company name on a cap, etc. Perhaps the person has a military, national, ethnic, gang or family tattoo. Many people sling their company security pass around their neck or leave it clipped to their belt when they leave the office. To an astute observer, these provide accurate intimate information such as their name, a date of birth, position in the company and sometimes their security classification. Others have their driver's licence, social security or medical card under a clear plastic cover on the inside of their wallet; when they pay at the cash register they display a large amount of very private information ranging from their full name, date of birth and residential address to the names of other family members.

If you are one of these people, please hide these cards deeper within your wallet or purse. A glance at your driver's licence immediately tells thieves two vital things—one, your address and two, you are not home.

Continuing with our scenario; your observations are undertaken very quickly and continue for a minute or two, while you are standing in the queue for your coffee. You survey the person's type of watch, jewellery (including necklaces displaying a star sign, a name or initials) make-up and the standard of their personal grooming. When all these are put together it allows you to make an assessment of whether the person is a professional, a tradesperson, a tourist, unemployed or salesperson, etc., very quickly. A brief assessment such as this is sometimes all that is required. Be confident with your gut feeling about a person when you make such an assessment. Sometimes you may get it wrong, but on most occasions you won't. Even when you do, you now have a complete list of new skills to use that will pave the way for a smooth and enjoyable interaction.

A similarly brief assessment may be undertaken if you are meeting a patient, customer or student for the first time. The assessment phase in these situations only takes a minute or two—it's not 100% accurate and it doesn't matter if you get it a bit wrong. As long as you remain flexible and adapt your conversation once you have engaged the secret-keeper, you will be well on the path to eliciting the type of information you are after.

At the other end of the spectrum are more in-depth and time consuming research and assessment phases. The secret-keeper may be a prospective client, business partner or business competitor; in these situations the research and assessment phase is critical and may involve developing a full profile of a person from every available source. The value of the information you are after will determine how much effort you want to invest.

You may or may not engage a private investigator. Though with a bit of effort, a lot can be learned about people before actually talking to them, via the internet through Facebook, LinkedIn, Google and company websites. An electoral roll or other public record may provide an address and a quick search on Google Earth may show you useful information about the person—the size of their house, the type of car they drive, whether there is a boat in the yard or they have highly manicured lawns or a pool. When all this type of information is added together, it starts to complete a picture about what type of person the secret-keeper is and can make for a very accurate assessment.

If a secret-keeper in your workplace has an office or workstation it will most likely have vital research information ready available for your casual observation—without breaking and entering! Items such as photos, qualifications and certificates, books, etc. can provide you an insight into the person.

Regardless of whether our research was undertaken over a minute or a month, before we decide on the hook and line, we need to determine what the secret-keeper's personality state is at the time of your first meeting.

The Secret-keeper's Personality State

This is not a technical personality assessment. You don't need to know about psychometric testing and personality-type profiling procedures; you can make a simple assessment based on your life experiences and observations of people over the years. What you are assessing is the secret-keeper's 'personality' at that time which combines mood and personality type and also takes into consideration the environment the secret-keeper is in when you make the assessment. It sounds complicated but it's actually very easy.

Some profilers and psychologists will have you believe that you are not qualified to make such an assessment and that without some very complicated personality profiling tools an accurate assessment cannot be conducted. Don't believe them! I think that most people are quite astute at assessing a person's personality state when they first meet or even just observe a person—this is a naturally honed human capability.

Stretching as far back as when humans first started to walk the planet, we have all successfully evolved from a background of being able to very quickly assess who was a threat, who was friendly, who we felt safe with, who was a good leader, who was a good provider and who we wanted to breed with and who we didn't. We humans usually get it right—those who didn't stopped breeding or were killed off in caves thousands of years ago—thanks, Dr Darwin! In addition to our evolutionary capabilities, we have individually developed our skills throughout our own lifetimes in families, social relationships and at work. This makes us pretty good at assessing others.

Even if you had access to a secret-keeper's recent technical personality profile, the person's demeanor may well be different from what you expected due to internal life factors and external environmental stimuli. For example, a person who was assessed in a personality type test as being 'more interested in ideas than social interaction. Quiet, contained, flexible and adaptive' [83] may be very outgoing and much more sociable than predicted because the person is excited, having a good day, just received a pay rise or is affected by drugs or alcohol.

This is because a person's mood and behavior will vary at different times and in divergent circumstances due to internal factors such as the amount of sleep, food or stress the person is under and also environmental stimuli, such as heat, cold, noise, etc. You may know of 'morning people' who spring into the day with exuberance as soon as they wake and then there is the rest of us who should be avoided until we have had our first cup of coffee! Internal and external stimuli can affect a secret-keeper's personality state, regardless of what their technical personality type is.

Just try to strike up a humorous conversation in a shopping mall with a parent who is holding a screaming baby or young child having a tantrum. I can assure you the wittiest comment won't tickle the funny bone of that parent in that situation. The most placid and understanding parent in that situation will have no sense of humor (at that time)—a trait not in their personality type. In that situation the only ones with a sense of humor are observing parents of older children and grandparents who have all endured many such performances, and strangely enough seem to enjoy witnessing others go through it!

Some examples of personality states:

- Highly motivated and busy
- Relaxed and laid back
- Tired and sleepy
- Energised
- Humorous and quick to laugh
- Serious and introverted
- Friendly and outgoing

These are just some of the many ways a secret-keeper may appear to you when making your assessment. Psychologists may shudder when reading such a list as these aren't technical psychometrically measurable personality states. However, I can verify that as an Intelligence tradecraft, this method works. As everyday people, we don't need to learn complex and complicated psychological tools. My advice is to also trust your 'gut' instinct on the type of person the secret-keeper is at the time you meet. When you combine all that you have learned from your research and made your observations of the secret-keeper, you should feel confident that you can make an accurate assessment.

STEP TWO: Engage the secret-keeper—hook, line and syncher

Once you've researched and made an assessment of the secret-keeper, the next step to unlocking hidden information is to successfully 'engage' the secret-keeper in conversation. We covered using the hook, line and syncher method in detail in *Part Three*.

'Engage' is the operative word and means more than just having a conversation; you need to really get the person talking and break down any dialogue resistance. The primary purpose of engaging the secret-keeper is to rapidly build a close and sharing rapport with the person and this rarely occurs during normal day-to-day conversations. At the end of your engaging conversation, the secret-keeper should feel a connection with you and have thoroughly enjoyed talking with you.

Based on your research (which may be a lengthy process or a quick scan of the environment), you should have an idea of what hook will be effective.

Additionally, your observation of the secret-keeper just before you meet should also provide you an insight into the person's current personality state and based on that, you should be able to psychologically mirror the secret-keeper when you first meet (demonstrating your shared emotional experience in that environment).

The engage step is about having a meaningful conversation and it's critical to really get the conversation flowing, not about the secret itself, but any mutually interesting subject. Don't worry or rush to make a connection, this will occur during the conversation as a result of using the hook, line and syncher method. We just want to get the flow of general information (about a common issue or subject) that places you both on the same side and feeling the same about the subject. Align yourself with the secret-keeper.

At this initial stage any conversation is better than no conversation; the secret-keeper will provide the information you need to direct the dialogue that will cause the person to feel emotionally closer to you and to want to talk with you further. It's through interpersonal exchanges that we make assessments about people and you can use your life skills to demonstrate just how 'likeable' you are! This may be reinforced through positive body language.

Using positive body language

- Friendly eye contact: Avoid looking around the room when either of you is speaking as it indicates you are not that interested. Without staring and freaking the person out, try to make the secret-keeper feel as though they are the most interesting person in the room. If you can do this, the secret-keeper will start to feel a connection with you.

- Avoid crossed arms and legs: This should be avoided as it can project that you are defensive or guarded.

- Use your head: Try to match the height of your head with the secret-keeper. Nod as the secret-keeper is talking to make it clear that what the person is saying is interesting and you agree.

- Be, or at least appear relaxed: Have a relaxed and open body posture. If you are nervous, which you may be, this is best concealed by relaxing your body and casually resting or anchoring any fidgeting arms or legs to a fixture such as a table top, the legs of a chair, etc. When people are nervous or appear stiff and cold, it's difficult to communicate with them as we ourselves are then not at our ease. Fight the urge to shrink and fold up. Relax yourself but don't encroach on the secret-keeper's personal space. This reflects self-assuredness.

- Lean: Slightly lean towards the secret-keeper when listening. Don't lean back as this may portray that you are arrogant or distant, but don't lean in too close, as this may appear intimidating or needy—both are undesirable. Use an 'interested' lean.

- Smile: People are naturally attracted to positive people. Smile when you meet and remain ready to laugh. Even if you psychologically mirror a frustrated secret-keeper (hence you are frustrated also), then steer the person towards a happier state, e.g. making light of the situation. But don't force a prolonged smile as it's almost impossible to fake a genuine smile, and a prolonged one will appear insincere. Use your normal smile, as people accept and feel more at ease with a friendly face.

- Avoid face touching: One of the signs of deceit is when a person regularly touches their face, particularly the nose as there is an increase of blood flow to the erectile tissue in the nose during stressful and anxious situations. If you touch your face regularly this may be perceived by the secret-keeper that you are being deceitful.

- Body mirroring: When two people are relating well during a conversation they naturally will adopt the same or similar body positions. To improve your interrelatedness, you may do this proactively by mirroring the secret-keeper. This should be done subtly and adjusted a short time after the person has changed as the conversation takes place. *A word of caution*: Almost everyone knows about body language and body mirroring, so you need to use this very carefully. If the secret-keeper identifies you are doing this, you will immediately lack credibility and stand out as insincere.

Remain flexible and adapt your psychological mirror during your conversation as the person may be different to your initial assessment or their mood at the time of the meeting may cause them to be different. There is also a vast difference between a person's public image in business and their personality. Even when it is insanely boring, keep the secret-keeper talking and contribute comments or statements that positively reinforce how similar you are. For obvious reasons, it's important to never argue with what a secret-keeper says.

Using faults to open vaults

Sincerity and credibility are two attributes a secret-keeper will be assessing when considering whether or not to discuss a secret with you. No one is perfect and when we meet a person who never admits any faults or problems, often we decide that the person is hiding something from us. This in turn makes us reticent to share information with the person.

To increase your credibility with a secret-keeper, you should feel free to share a mistake or two (even fabricated ones) during your conversation. If the secret-keeper shares a regretful incident or mistake, this is a prime time to insert your own similar experience. This will assist in bringing you closer, improve your credibility and increase your human side from the secret-keeper's perspective.

Follow the hook, line and syncher process to fully engage the person as you continue to have a general rapport-building conversation. When you feel the secret-keeper is relaxed and conversing with ease and you gauge there is a positive interpersonal connection, it's time to move the conversation towards the information you are seeking and access the hidden information.

STEP THREE: Access the hidden information—segue to secrecy

While the secret-keeper should be thoroughly enjoying the engaging conversation, it certainly won't be providing you with the information you require. Now you need to direct the general conversation to the area of the secret, without unsettling the positive interpersonal dynamics. How easy this is will depend primarily on how emotionally close you have become and how much the person trusts and likes you.

If you have used the techniques explained so far in this book you should be well on your way at this point to transitioning smoothly to accessing information based on the close rapport you have developed. However, regardless of how good the rapport is, you can't be having an engaging general conversation about the public transport system, personal relationships or a major news issue and then suddenly ask a pointed question focused on the information the person is keeping secret. Even if you have really connected with the person, an abrupt question about the secret may shock the secret-keeper and cause the person to raise their defences. This can influence the person to keep the conversation at a superficial level, or worse still reflect on whether you have a hidden agenda—which of course you do.

Even when secret-keepers know you are trying to access their hidden information in order to help them, a stark question like this hands conversational control over to them and they can then prevent your access. We don't want that. To achieve a smooth transition, as the general conversation is taking place look for conversational gates or *segues* (pronounced 'segways') that you can use to steer the conversation to the secret subject area.

Your goal should be for the secret-keeper to voluntarily tell you what you want to know without you having to ask any direct questions about the hidden information. By establishing a close rapport and then using conversation gates or segues, the secret-keeper will feel a connection with you and the secret naturally just seems to come up in conversation. Remember, there is a natural urge for secret-keepers to share and this process simply facilitates the pathway for the information to flow to you.

On most occasions during the engage phase you will learn enough information to segue your way to the secret subject area. However, when this doesn't occur it's possible to ask general and indirect broad questions about the secret area— not the secret itself. We want to avoid asking direct questions as these are too abrupt, may spook the person and will remain in the secret-keeper's mind well after the conversation has ended.

As you are carefully directing the conversation around to the secret area, the secret-keeper will react in one of two ways:

1. If the person feels uncomfortable as the conversation steers towards the secret area there may be an obvious signal as the secret-keeper abruptly defects the conversation to a new topic. Or you may notice

the secret-keeper's body language subtly start to change—crossed arms (defensive), stiffened body or eyes start darting around the room (avoiding your eye contact and looking to escape). These are signals that the secret-keeper is starting to disengage. It's a sign that we need to look for and react to.

2. Employing the same level of care used to approach the secret, we now withdraw from that area and naturally move the conversation to a safe area by reintroducing a topic where the secret-keeper was relating well to you (a syncher) or any new point of mutual interest. This doesn't mean you can't approach the secret again later during your time together, or preferably at a later meeting.

3. The second response may be positive and the secret-keeper may start to communicate the hidden information. If this occurs, learn as much as you can by listening. Try not to ask questions as this may stall the secret-keeper. If the secret-keeper pauses and appears to be reconsidering whether to continue revealing the secret, depending on the situation you may find it useful to:

   • Use normalising statements such as:

     • 'Well, anyone in your situation would feel that way.'
     • 'I can fully understand why you feel ...'
     • 'Accidents like this just happen sometimes.'
     • 'There are plenty of other people in the same situation.'
     • 'It can be hard growing up.' (to a teenager)
     • 'It's just a mistake.'

   • Minimise the significance of the information: 'That's interesting but I wouldn't be too worried. This can just be between us; it's not like it's Wikileaks. It's just two people talking.'

   • Increase emotional empathy: 'I know this is difficult for you to talk about, but sometimes it feels better to offload...'

   • Share a similar secret of your own: This will increase the pressure to share (quid pro quo).

You may recall from the section *Secret Attractions, Secret Relationships and White Bears* that when a secret is finally unlocked the information flows more freely than if it had not been a secret in the first place. So one aspect we need to be aware of is that once we unlock a person's secret and they send a large amount of previously confidential information our way, we need to be prepared for how best to handle the information and also the person. Additionally, once a person has shared their secret with you they are more likely to talk to you about it again.

In summary, the access phase is focused on naturally opening up a conversation about the secret without asking the secret-keeper any direct questions. To do this it's best to use segues to steer the conversation to the hidden information. If this approach is not working, then broad indirect questions about the general secret area may be used.

You can practise using segues to steer conversations every day even when you are not trying to unlock a secret. You will be surprised at how much you can control and direct a conversation without the other person realising.

STEP FOUR: Divert the conversation

Once the secret-keeper has shared the information, it's critical that the person doesn't feel violated or trespassed upon as a result of discussing the information with you. This is particularly important when using these skills to assist a person to open up in order to provide better support. Remember that if a person is keeping a secret, for any number of reasons, it is important to them.

Depending on the nature of the secret, when it is shared the person will sometimes feel a sense of regret and vulnerability, often after the conversation. The person may also feel used or that they have been betrayed, or may have betrayed themself or others by sharing the information. Regardless of the circumstances or motives for accessing a secret, we always want the secret-keeper to feel positive about the interaction, even when the person reflects back on what has been shared. To do this, it's imperative to round off the interaction and take the conversation well away from the secret area. This will serve to minimise any internal conflict the person may feel and also ensure the person is willing to discuss that secret or another secret with you in future.

Strangely, people are mostly consistent with the way they approach someone a second time. If the first meeting ended in a heated way, the greeting will most often be tainted by that. Similarly, if people separate on a positive note, when they meet again the relationship will commence from that very point.

One of the reasons for this is that despite the passage of time and circumstances that may affect each individual's mood, nothing has occurred to actually alter the relationship in the intervening period. As such, the departing emotion endures and may be reignited when the two meet again. This may all change once the second interaction is underway; however, most often the start of a second meeting is influenced by the way the first one ended.

Notwithstanding the secret-keeper learning something unfavorable about you in the intervening period, ending the first conversation in a close and positive way will set the mood for the commencement of the second meeting. We have learned that people share information with those they like and those they have an emotional link with. As such, by the end of the first meeting we want this to be prominent in the secret-keeper's mind, not that information was shared, so when you meet again the conversation is initiated just as it left off.

If during the intervening period, the secret-keeper reassesses that too much information was shared, the person will be more guarded when you next meet, but the departing emotion will still prevail. So we need to accomplish two things in the divert phase:

1. After the hidden information has been shared, divert the conversation away from that subject. If you haven't asked any direct questions this should occur quite readily.

2. Take the conversation to a happy and safe place for the secret-keeper to set the tone for the commencement of the next interaction.

The divert phase should be used even where the secret-keeper has not shared any information. By adopting this process, you should be well placed to have a subsequent attempt. Even if you expect to never see the person again, you don't know what circumstances may bring you together again. By completing the process with the divert phase, you will be placed favorably in the mind of that person when you next meet. Additionally when you meet you should have some synchers from the first meeting to use to take the secret-keeper to the closest and most sharing point of your last encounter.

PART FOUR KEY POINTS

READ is a handy acronym for an elicitation model which sets out four easy steps to follow when you are attempting to unlock hidden information. It can be used for both long and short term elicitation and in both direct and indirect elicitation processes:

Research and assess the secret-keeper.

- Research: Learn as much as possible about the secret-keeper. Considering the circumstances, this may vary from a couple of minutes to a couple of months.

- Assess: Assess the personality state of the secret-keeper in the environment when you are about to meet.

Engage the secret-keeper—hook, line and syncher.

- Hook: Based on your assessment, use psychological mirroring and an appropriate hook to initiate a conversation about a subject of mutual interest.

- Line: Then cast your elicitation line or lines to rapidly build rapport and bring you closer to the secret-keeper.

- Syncher: Take note of parts of the conversation that the secret-keeper reacts positively to, or suddenly starts sharing information about. These synchers can be used when next you meet, to recreate the secret-keeper's positive and/or close emotional 'feelings' from the previous encounter.

Access the hidden information—segue to secrecy: To subtly access the subject of the hidden information, during the conversation look for conversational gates or segues that you can use to steer the conversation to the secret subject area. Avoid asking direct questions. If you notice that the secret-keeper starts to disengage from you or makes it clear that the subject is off limits, continue to use lines and build rapport but move away from that subject area. However, if the information starts to

flow learn as much as you can and set the stage for another meeting by taking note of synchers at this intimate sharing level.

Divert the conversation away from the sensitive subject area, so that the shared information is not prominent in the mind of the secret-keeper after the meeting has ended. Create a happy ending so the secret-keeper will be predisposed to commence your next meeting the same way.

GO FOR IT!

Congratulations! You are now armed with the knowledge you need to find out all sorts of information from all sorts of people. However, this new knowledge needs to be put into practice so it can develop into an effective skill. This isn't a daunting task; in fact, it's fun! You will be amazed when you use these skills just how much information people will share with you. I encourage you to practise as often as possible, starting with simple conversations in everyday situations.

For example, you may be purchasing something from a store and you engage the salesperson using these techniques. Your goal is to extract as much information about the salesperson as you can. You may learn how long the person has worked there, the person's salary, whether s/he is married, even the home address. Why? Because it's great practice and if you engage the secret-keeper properly, when you leave they will have thoroughly enjoyed the conversation and be left thinking what a nice person you are and hoping to talk with you again!

You can do this at bus stops, in the workplace, on trains, with taxi drivers, at parties, etc. There is no downside to these sorts of activities as both you and the secret-keeper should enjoy the process as you build your skills and confidence.

You are now privy to some of the most cutting edge and effective elicitation techniques and how to apply them to your personal and professional life to unlock secrets; but don't tell anyone—keep it a secret!

NOTES

1. The book *Lie Catcher: Become a Human Lie Detector in Under 60 Minutes*, also published as *Detect Deceit* (USA & Canada) can be purchased online from Big Sky Publishing (www.bigskypublishing.com. au).

2. *Sixty Minutes* (Australia) report dated 18 November 2011. According to the interviewee, Mr Richard Clarke (who was Counter-Terrorism Chief under both Presidents Clinton and Bush), countries such as China are stealing not only military secrets but also raiding classified corporate information. This information is then provided by the Chinese government to Chinese Corporations, who then compete commercially with the companies whose secrets have been stolen. AT: http://60minutes.9msn. com/article.aspx?id=8376293

3. A VriJ et al (2002). 'Characteristics of Secrets and the Frequency, Reasons and Effects of Secret Keeping and Disclosure'. *Journal of Community and Applied Social Psychology*. Wiley and Sons, United Kingdom.

4. A VriJ et al (2002). 'Characteristics of Secrets and the Frequency, Reasons and Effects of Secret Keeping and Disclosure'. *Journal of Community and Applied Social Psychology*. Wiley and Sons, United Kingdom.

5. G Margolis (1974). *The Psychology of Keeping Secrets*. International Review of Psychoanalysis.

6. Pennebaker, J.W., Colder, M.,&Sharp, L. K. (1990). Pennebaker, J.W., Kiecolt-Glaser, J. K., & Glaser, R. (1988).
    Petrie, K. J., Booth, R. J., Pennebaker, J.W., Davison, K. P., & Thomas, M. G. (1995).

7. For example, Schwartz, G. E. (1990) 'Psychology of repression and health: a systems approach'. IN: J.L. Singer, *Repression and disassociation: Implications for personality theory. Psychopathology and Health*. Chicago. The University of Chicago. Scarf, M. (2004) *Secrets, Lies, Betrayals How the Body Holds Secrets of a Life, and How to Unlock Them*. Random House

8. Description adapted from Kelly, A. E. (2002) *The Psychology of Secrets. Bok. S. (1989) Secrets: On the ethics of concealment and revelation. New York.*

9. Norton, R., Feldman, C., & Tafoya, D (1974) 'Risk Parameters across Types of Secrets'. *Journal of Counselling Psychology*.

10. Schwolsky, E. (2001) 'Keeping Secrets'. *American Journal of Nursing*. Lippincott, Williams & Wilkins. Some elements of the stated example have been changed so the child cannot be identified.

11. For example, Australia, the United Kingdom, the United States, New Zealand, Japan. Seventeen-year patents exist in Canada.

12. Hannah, D.R., (2006) 'Keeping Trade Secrets Secret'. *IN: MITSloan Management Review*

13. BBC News (2006) at http://news.bbc.co.uk/2/hi/5152740.stm

14. Kaplan, E. (1987). *Development of the sense of separateness and autonomy during middle childhood and adolescence.* Mahler, M. S., Pine, F., and Bergman, A. (1975*). The Psychological Birth of the Human Infant.* Basic Books, New York. Meares, R., & Orlay, W (1988) 'On Self Boundary: A Study of the Development of the Concept of Secrecy'. *British Journal of Medical Psychology*, United Kingdom.

15. Meares, R., & Orlay, W (1988) 'On Self Boundary: A Study of the Development of the Concept of Secrecy'. *British Journal of Medical Psychology*, United Kingdom.

16. Watson AJ, Valtin R (1997) 'Secrecy in Middle Childhood'. *International Journal of Behavioural Development*.

17. Craig, D.R. (2011). *Lie Catcher: Become Human Lie Detector in Under 60 Minutes*. Big Sky Publishing, Sydney Australia.

18. Last, U (1991) 'Secrets and Reasons for Secrecy Among School-Aged Children: Development Trends and Gender Differences'. *Journal of Genetic Psychology.* Hebrew University of Jerusalem. Blos, P. (1967). *The second individuation process of adolescence. Psychoannual Study Child* 22: 162–168.

19. Blos, P. (1979). *The AdolescentPassage*. International Universities Press,New York.

20. Craig, D.R. (2011) *Lie Catcher: Become Human Lie Detector in Under 60 Minutes*. Big Sky Publishing, Sydney Australia

21. Frij, T. (2005) *Keeping Secrets; Quality, Quantity and Consequences*. PhD Thesis Vu University Amsterdam.

22. Kelly, A. E., (2011) IN: *The Two Types of Secrets by Sykes, C. AT: www. purematters.com*

23. Settle, M. (2009) BBC Radio Four, *The Secrets that People Keep from their Nearest and Dearest t*http://news.bbc.co.uk/2/hi/8366140.stm

24. Norton, R., Feldman, C., & Tafoya, D (1974) 'Risk Parameters across Types of Secrets'. *Journal of Counselling Psychology.*

25. Britton, G. R. A., Brinthaupt, J., Stehle, J. M. and James, G. D. (2004), *Comparison of Self-Reported Smoking and Urinary Cotinine Levels in a Rural Pregnant Population. Journal of Obstetric, Gynecologic, & Neonatal Nursing. United States.*

26. As reported anonymously in the study by Norton, R., Feldman, C., & Tafoya, D (1974) *Risk Parameters across Types of Secrets. Journal of Counselling Psychology*

27. Caughlin, J. P et al. (2000) *Intrafamily Secrets in various Family Configurations: A Communication Boundary Management Perspective. Communication Studies United States*

28. Vangelisti, A. L., (1994) *Family Secrets: forms, functions and correlates. Journal of Social and personal Relationships.*

29. IrabetBlack, E. (1998) *The Secret Life of Families.* Bantam Books, New York

30. Case reported to the author (2012). The names and identity of the people have been protected, and the matter was eventually reported to the police by one of the family members.

31. An inference should not be drawn that being a paedophile was directly linked to Peter being gay. However, in the reported case, the person was both gay and a paedophile.

32. Legal advice should be sought before any such strategy is attempted, to ensure that the elicitation of that type of information in that environment is conducted within the relevant laws. The author does not in any way support the illegal procurement of sensitive information from any source.

33. Computerworld UK reporter (2008) *Most IT staff would steal company secrets*: survey AT: www.computerworlduk.com. Survey conducted by Cyber-Ark.

34. Hill, C. E., Thompson, B. J., Cogar, M. C., & Denman, D. W. (1993). *Beneath the surface of long-term therapy: Therapist and client report*

of their own and each other's covert processes. Journal of Counselling Psychology.

35. Delaney-Black,V.,Chiodo, L.M., Hannigan,J.H., Greenwald, M.K., Patterson, G., Huestis, M.A., Ager,J. & Sokol, R.J. (2009): *Just Say 'I Don't': Lack of Concordance Between Teen Report and Biological Measures of Drug* Use American Academy of Paediatrics. Only two categories of information could be divulged within the terms of the Agreement - child abuse or plans to hurt themselves or others.

36. Britton, G. R. A., Brinthaupt, J., Stehle, J. M. and James, G. D. (2004), *Comparison of Self-Reported Smoking and Urinary Cotinine Levels in a Rural Pregnant Population. Journal of Obstetric, Gynecologic, & Neonatal Nursing. United States.*

37. Kelly, A. E. (2002) *The Psychology of Secrets*. New York. Specifically, five clients were too afraid to express their feelings; three were too ashamed or embarrassed; three that revealing the secret would show a lack of progress to the therapist.

38. Rettner, R (2012) *1 in 10 Smokers Keep the Habit Secret from Doctors.* IN: My Health News Daily.

39. Olsen, J. Barefoot, J.C. & Strickland, L.H. (1976) *What the Shadow Knows: Person Perception in a Surveillance Situation IN Journal of Personality and Social Psychology.*

40. Bellman, B. (1984) *The Language of Secrecy*. New Brunswick, Rutgers University Press.

41. Wegner, D.M, Lane, J. D. & Dimitri, S. (1994) *The Allure of Secret Relationships IN: Journal of Personality and Social Psychology*

42. Jaffe, E. (2006) *The Science Behind Secrets*. Association for Psychological Science

43. Research conducted by Wegner in 1987 – published results in Journal of Personality and Social Psychology

44. Ichiyama, M. A., et al (1993). *Self-concealment and Correlates of Adjustment in College Students*. Journal of College Student Psychotherapy

45. Saffer, J. B., Sansone, P., & Gentry, J. (1979). *The Awesome Burden upon the Child who Must Keep a Family Secret*. Child Psychiatry and Human Development.

46. Larson, D. G., & Chastain, R. L. (1990). *Self-concealment: Conceptualization, Measurement, and Health Implications.* Journal of Social and Clinical Psychology. Guilford Press Periodicals.

47. Cole, S.W., et al (1996). *Elevated Physical Health Risk Among Gay Men who Conceal their Homosexual Identity.* Psychological Association, Health Psychology.

48. Spiegel D. Et al (1989) *Effect of Psychosocial Treatment on Survival of Patients with Metastatic Breast Cancer.*

49. Some believe that Dr Pennebaker's research is more focused upon 'not disclosing traumatic events' as opposed to 'secrecy' – however, such a proposition depends upon the description used to define secrecy itself. Dr Pennebaker's work fits with the description used by this book.

50. Pennebaker, J., W (2005) *Writing to Heal.* University of Texas at www.utexas.edu/features/2005/writing/

51. Also see Dr Pennebaker's book 'Writing to Heal' for more detail

52. Holmberg, U. & Christianson, S. A. (2002) *Murders and Sexual Offenders Experiences of Police Interviews and their Inclination to Admit or Deny Crimes.* In: Behavioural Sciences and the Law.

53. Shepherd, E. (1991) *Ethical Interviewing. Policing and Shepherd, E (1993) Aspects of Police Interviewing. Issues in Criminological and Legal Psychology. The British Psychological Society. Leicester England . Ord, B et al (2004) Investigative Interviewing Explained. Butterworths Australia*

54. http://www.thefreedictionary.com/empathy.

55. Koehnken, G., Milne, R., Memon, A., Bull, R. (1999) *The Cognitive Interview – a meta-analysis. Psychology Crime and Law.*

56. Bull, R. (1991) *Police Investigative Interviewing* in: Memon, A. & Bull, R. *Handbook of the Psychology of Interviewing*, Wiley, Chichester

57. At the time (2000), the operative was using the recording when public speaking and teaching communications skills – as an example of what not to do!

58. These are termed Other Focused Lies and are further explaination of this in my book 'Lie Catcher / Detect Deceit: Become a Human Lie Detector in Under 60 Minutes'

59. VriJ, A. et al (2002). *Characteristics of Secrets and the Frequency, Reasons and Effects of Secret Keeping and Disclosure. Journal of*

Community and Applied Social Psychology. Wiley and Sons, United Kingdom.

60. Finkenauer, C., & Rime, B. (1998) *Socially Shared Emotional Experience Kept Secret: Differential Characteristics and Consequences. Journal of Social and Clinical Psychology*

61. VriJ, A. et al (2002). *Characteristics of Secrets and the Frequency, Reasons and Effects of Secret Keeping and Disclosure. Journal of Community and Applied Social Psychology. Wiley and Sons, United Kingdom.*

62. The number of Round One participants, in the two round study where questionnaires were filled out 4 months apart. I also doubt very much that the remaining students, didn't have any secret information at all.

63. Averaged Round One results interpreted from VriJ, A. et al (2002) [IBID] and other research into the proportionate disclosure of secrets.

64. Averaged percentages of several studies reflected these proportioned results.

65. Goldstein, J.,N., Martin, J. S., Caildini, B, R. (2008) *Yes 50 Scientifically Proven Ways to be Persuasive. Free Press New York.*

66. Garner, R., (2005) *What's in a name? Persuasion perhaps. Journal of Consumer Psychology*

67. Maddux,W.,W., Mullen, E., & Galinsky, A.,D., (2008) *Chameleons bake bigger pies and take bigger pieces: Strategic behavioural mimicry facilitates negotiation outcomes* Journal of Experimental Social Psychology. Tanner, R. et al (2008). *Of Chameleons and Consumption: The Impact of Mimicry on Choice and Preferences* Journal of Consumer Research

68. For ways to accurately identify a real from a false smile see my first book *Lie Catcher / Detect Deceit: Become a Human Lie Detector in Under 60 Minutes.*

69. Simmel, G. (1950) *The Secret and the Secret Society* IN: K. W. Woiff. *The Sociology of Georg Simmel. Free Press New York. Richardson, L., (1988) Secrecy and Status: The social construction of forbidden relationships. American Sociological Review.*

70. Bellman, B. (1984) *The Language of Secrecy.* New Brunswick, Rutgers University Press

71. Regan, D.,T., (1971) *Effects of a Favour and Liking on Compliance. Journal of Experimental Psychology*

72. Finkenauer, c. (1988) *Secrets: Types, Determinants, Functions and Consequences*. Unpublished doctoral dissertation, University of Louvain Belgium.

73. Story by James Kanter of the *New York Times* (August 2009) is just one readily available example. www.nytimes.com/2009/09/01/business/energy-environment/01iht-bulb.html

74. A Knishinski (1982). 'The effects of scarcity of material and exclusivity of information on industrial buyer perceived risk in provoking a purchase decision'. In Gilbert, D. T, Fiske, S.T., Lindzey, G. (1998) *The Handbook of Social Psychology* McGraw-Hill New York.

75. A Knishinski (1982). 'The effects of scarcity of material and exclusivity of information on industrial buyer perceived risk in provoking a purchase decision'. In DT Gilbert, ST Fiske, Lindzey, G. (1998) *The Handbook of Social Psychology* McGraw-Hill New York

76. S Cameron (2010). *On the Farm: Robert William Pickton and the Tragic Story of Vancouver's Missing Women*. Knopf Canada

77. A Cameron (2010). *On the Farm: Robert William Pickton and the Tragic Story of Vancouver's Missing Women*. Knopf Canada. See also links at CBC News at http://www.cbc.ca/news/background/pickton/; http://www.cbc.ca/news/canada/british-columbia/story/2012/04/09/bc-survivor-missing-women-inquiry.html.

78. To make the transcript easier to follow, I have added punctuation and filled in some logical blanks in the conversation. A full unedited transcript can be found at http://www2.canada.com/story.html?id=3374511. Also see *A Serial Killers Own Words: The Pickton Transcript* published by the *Vancouver Sun* on 7 August 2010. Videos of this interaction are also readily found on You Tube.

79. CBC News 9 December 2007. AT: http://www.cbc.ca/news/canada/story/2007/12/09/pickton-verdict.html

80. http://www.theglobeandmail.com/news/national/decision-not-to-try-pickton-on-20-more-charges-outrages-families/article1377465/.

81. CTV News 16 November 2010. AT http://www.ctvnews.ca/serial-killer-robert-pickton-s-trial-cost-102-million-1.575485.

82. The optimum position for interviewing is 10 to 2 position. Schollum, M (2005). *Investigative Interviewing: The Literature*. Office of the New Zealand Police Commissioner.

83. Myers-Briggs Type Indicator (INTP). Katherine C. Briggs & Isabel Briggs Myers Type Indicator test, Australian Council for Educational Research Limited (1999). This example is not meant to be critical of such tests, but used to highlight that at different temporal locations, individual moods can affect the way people engage with others.

BIBLIOGRAPHY

Bradshaw J (1996). *Family Secrets. The Path from Shame to Healing.* Random House Publishing Group.

Bellman B (1984). *The Language of Secrecy.* New Brunswick, Rutgers University Press.

Blos P (1967). 'The second individuation process of adolescence'. *Psychoannual Study Child.* 22: 162–168.

Blos P (1979). *The Adolescent Passage.* International Universities Press, New York.

Bok S (1989). *Secrets: On the ethics of concealment and revelation.* New York. Vintage Books.

Britton GRA, Brinthaupt J, Stehle JM and James GD (2004). 'Comparison of Self-Reported Smoking and Urinary Cotinine Levels in a Rural Pregnant Population'. *Journal of Obstetric, Gynecologic, & Neonatal Nursing.* United States.

Brown LK and DeMaio DM (1992). *The Impact of Secrets in Haemophilia and HIV Disorders.* Journal of Psychological Oncology, The Haworth Press.

Bull R (1991). 'Police Investigative Interviewing'. In Memon, A. & Bull, R. *Handbook of the Psychology of Interviewing,* Wiley, Chichester.

Caildini RB (2001). *Influence: Science and Practice.* Allyn & Bacon, Needham Heights, MA.

Cameron S (2010). *On the Farm: Robert William Pickton and the Tragic Story of Vancouver's Missing Women.* Knopf, Canada.

Caughlin JP, Golish T, Olson L, Sargent J, Cook J and Petronio (2000). *Intrafamily Secrets in various Family Configurations: A Communication Boundary Management Perspective.* Communication Studies (Summer ed). United States.

Cole SW, Kemeny ME, Taylor SE, & Visscher BR (1996). *Elevated Physical Health Risk Among Gay Men who Conceal their Homosexual Identity.* American Psychological Association, Health Psychology. www.cancer-network.org/media/pdf/cancer_gay_men_disclosure_1996

Delaney-Black V, Chiodo LM, Hannigan JH, Greenwald MK, Patterson G, Huestis MA, Ager J & Sokol RJ (2009). *Just Say 'I Don't': Lack of Concordance Between Teen Report and Biological Measures of Drug Use*. American Academy of Paediatrics.

Eagly AH & Chaiken S (1998). 'Attitude Structure and Function'. In Gilbert D, Fiske, S and Lindsay G. *Handbook of Social Psychology*, MacGraw-Hill, New York.

Finkenauer C, & Rime B (1998). 'Socially Shared Emotional Experience Kept Secret: Differential Characteristics and Consequences'. *Journal of Social and Clinical Psychology*.

Finkenauer C, Engles RC & Meeus W (2002). 'Keeping Secrets from Parents: Advantages and Disadvantages of Secrecy in Adolescence'. *Journal of Youth and Adolescence*.

Frij T (2005). *Keeping Secrets; Quality, Quantity and Consequences*. PhD Thesis Vu University Amsterdam.

Garner R, (2005). 'What's in a name? Persuasion perhaps'. *Journal of Consumer Psychology*.

Gilbert DT, Fiske ST, Lindzey G (1998). *The Handbook of Social Psychology*. McGraw-Hill New York.

Goldstein JN, Martin JS, Caildini BR (2008). *Yes. 50 Scientifically Proven Ways to be Persuasive*. Free Press New York.

Hannah DR, (2006). *Keeping Trade Secrets Secret*. In MITSloan Management Review.

Hill CE, Thompson BJ, Cogar MC, & Denman DW (1993). 'Beneath the Surface of Long-term Therapy: Therapist and Client Report of their own and each other's Covert Processes'. *Journal of Counselling Psychology*.

Holmberg U & Christianson, SA (2002). 'Murders and Sexual Offenders Experiences of Police Interviews and their Inclination to Admit or Deny Crimes'. *Behavioural Sciences and the Law*.

Ichiyama MA, Colbert D, Laramore H, Heim M, Carone K & Schmidt J (1993). 'Self-concealment and Correlates of Adjustment in College Students'. *Journal of College Student Psychotherapy*. Also at www.tandfonline.com.

IrabetBlack, E (1998). *The Secret Life of Families*. Bantam Books, New York.

Inbau FE, Reid JE, Buckley JP & Jayne, BC (2001). *Criminal Interrogation and Confessions.* Aspen, Gaithersburg, MD.

Jaffe E (2006). *The Science Behind Secrets*. Association for Psychological Science—Observer Article AT: http://www.psychologicalscience.org/observer/getArticle.cfm?id=2015.

Kaplan E (1987). 'Development of the sense of separateness and autonomy during middle childhood and adolescence'. In Bloom-Feshbach, J, and Bloom-Feshbach, S (eds.), *The Psychology of Separation and Loss*. Jossey-Bass, San Francisco, CA.

Keane, C (2008). 'Don't Ask, Don't Tell'. *Journal of Management Enquiry*, Sage Publications, Canada.

Kelly AE (2002). *The Psychology of Secrets*. New York: Kluwer Academic / Plenum Publishers.

Kelly AE, (2011). *The Two Types of Secrets* by Sykes, C. AT: www.purematters.com.

Kent R (2007). 'Secrets and Lies'. *Nursing Standard* 25–31 July. RCN Publishing Company.

Knishinski A (1982). *The effects of scarcity of material and exclusivity of information on industrial buyer perceived risk in provoking a purchase decision*. Doctoral dissertation. Arizona State University.

Koehnken G, Milne R, Memon A, Bull R (1999). 'The Cognitive Interview: A meta-analysis'. *Psychology Crime and Law*.

Larson DG & Chastain RL (1990). 'Self-concealment: Conceptualization, Measurement, and Health Implications'. *Journal of Social and Clinical Psychology*. Guilford Press Periodicals.

Last U (1991). 'Secrets and Reasons for Secrecy Among School-Aged Children: Development Trends and Gender Differences'. *Journal of Genetic Psychology.* Hebrew University of Jerusalem.

Lehmiller JJ (2009). *Secret Romantic Relationships: Consequences for personal and Relational Well-Being.* Society for Personality and Social Pyschology.

Maddux WW, Mullen E & Galinsky AD (2008). 'Chameleons bake bigger pies and take bigger pieces: Strategic behavioural mimicry facilitates negotiation outcomes'. *Journal of Experimental Social Psychology*.

Margolis G (1974). *The Psychology of Keeping Secrets*. International Review of Psychoanalysis.

Mahler MS, Pine F and Bergman A (1975). *The Psychological Birth of the Human Infant*. Basic Books, New York.

Meares R & Orlay W (1988). 'On Self Boundary: A Study of the Development of the Concept of Secrecy'. *British Journal of Medical Psychology*. United Kingdom.

National Women's History Museum (2007). *A History of Women in Industry* at www.nwhm.org/online-exhibits/industry.

Norton R, Feldman C & Tafoya D (1974). 'Risk Parameters across Types of Secrets'. *Journal of Counseling Psychology*.

Olsen J, Barefoot JC & Strickland LH (1976). 'What the Shadow Knows: Person Perception in a Surveillance Situation'. *Journal of Personality and Social Psychology*

Ord B, Shaw G and Green T (2004). *Investigative Interviewing Explained*. Butterworths, Australia.

Pennebaker JW (2005). *Writing to Heal*. University of Texas at www.utexas.edu/features/2005/writing/.

Pennebaker JW (1989). 'Confession, Inhibition and Disease'. *Advances in Experimental Social Psychology*.

Pennebaker JW, (1990). *Opening up: the Healing Powers of Confiding in Others*. Morrow, New York.

Pennebaker JW, Beall SK (1986). 'Confronting a Traumatic Event: Toward an Understanding of Inhibition and Disease'. *Journal of Abnormal Psychology*.

Pennebaker JW (1997). 'Writing about Emotional Experiences as a Therapeutic Process'. *Psychological Science*. US.

Pennebaker JW, Colder M & Sharp LK (1990). 'Accelerating the Coping Process'. *Journal of Personality and Social Psychology*.

Pennebaker JW, Kiecolt-Glaser JK & Glaser R (1988). 'Disclosure of Traumas and Immune Function: Health Implications for Psychotherapy'. *Journal of Consulting and Clinical Psychology*.

Petrie KJ, Booth RJ, Pennebaker JW, Davison KP & Thomas MG (1995). 'Disclosure of Trauma and Immune Response to a Hepatitis B Vaccination Program'. *Journal of Consulting and Clinical Psychology*.

Regan DT (1971). 'Effects of a Favour and Liking on Compliance'. *Journal of Experimental Psychology*.

Rettner R (2012). '1 in 10 Smokers Keep the Habit Secret from Doctors'. My Health News Daily at: http://www.myhealthnewsdaily.com

Richardson L (1988). 'Secrecy and Status: The social construction of forbidden relationships'. *American Sociological Review*.

Saffer JB, Sansone P & Gentry J. (1979). 'The Awesome Burden upon the Child who Must Keep a Family Secret'. *Child Psychiatry and Human Development*, also at www.ncbi.nlm.nih.gov/pubmed/467129.

Scarf M (2004). *Secrets, Lies, Betrayals: How the Body Holds Secrets of a Life, and How to Unlock Them*. Random House.

Schollum M (2005). *Investigative Interviewing: The Literature*. Office of the New Zealand Police Commissioner.

Schwolsky E (2001). 'Keeping Secrets'. *American Journal of Nursing*. Lippincott, Williams & Wilkins.

Settle M (2009). 'The Secrets that People Keep from their Nearest and Dearest'. http://news.bbc.co.uk/2/hi/8366140.stm.

Shepherd E (1993). 'Aspects of Police Interviewing'. *Issues in Criminological and Legal Psychology*. The British Psychological Society. Leicester England.

Simmel G (1950). 'The Secret and the Secret Society'. In: KW Wolff. *The Sociology of Georg Simmel*. Free Press New York.

Spiegel D, Bloom JR, Kraemer HC, Gottheil E (1989). *Effect of Psychosocial Treatment on Survival of Patients with Metastatic Breast Cancer*. Department of Psychiatry and Behavioural Sciences, Stanford University School of Medicine, California.

Tanner R et al (2008). 'Of Chameleons and Consumption: The Impact of Mimicry on Choice and Preferences'. *Journal of Consumer Research*. US.

Tisseron S (2002). 'The Weight of the Family Secret'. *Queensland Quarterly*, United Kingdom.

Vangelisti AL (1994). 'Family Secrets: forms, functions and correlates'. *Journal of Social and Personal Relationships*.

VriJ A, Nunkoosing K, Paterson, B Oosterwegel, A and Soukara S (2002). 'Characteristics of Secrets and the Frequency, Reasons and Effects of Secret Keeping and Disclosure'. *Journal of Community and Applied Social Psychology*. Wiley and Sons, United Kingdom.

Watson AJ, Valtin R (1997). 'Secrecy in Middle Childhood'. *International Journal of Behavioural Development*.

Wegner DM, Lane JD & Dimitri S (1994). *'The Allure of Secret Relationships'*. *Journal of Personality and Social Psychology*.

ABOUT THE AUTHOR

Dr David Craig achieved his doctorate in law by completing international research of undercover programs in Australia, the United States, Canada, the United Kingdom and the Netherlands. During his 22 year career as a sworn federal agent, he was deployed in several covert policing roles for the Australian Federal Police. He has provided undercover tactics and management training in Australia and to overseas agencies.

As a Detective Superintendent, Dr Craig commanded more traditional significant investigations against organised crime and terrorism, such as the Bali 2 Bombings in 2005 and the Biological Attack on the Indonesian Embassy in Canberra in 2005. He has also been deployed to East Timor as part of the United Nations in 2002. In 2011, he completed 12 months in Afghanistan as part of NATO forces efforts in that country.

Dr Craig has now retired from the Australian Federal Police. He may be contacted through Big Sky Publishing in Sydney.